MEET
THE AUTHORS
AND
ILLUSTRATORS
VOLUME TWO

MEET
THE AUTHORS
AND
ILLUSTRATORS

VOLUME TWO

60 Creators of Favorite Children's Books Talk About Their Work

BY DEBORAH KOVACS AND JAMES PRELLER

SCHOLASTIC
PROFESSIONAL BOOKS

NEW YORK • TORONTO • LONDON • AUCKLAND • SYDNEY

For Sarah and Lucy
DEBORAH KOVACS

For my brothers and sisters: Neal, Bill, Barbara, John, Al, and Jean
JAMES PRELLER

Design by Jacqueline Swensen
Cover illustration by Delana Bettoli
Photo research by Donna Frankland, Grace How, Daniella Jo Nilva, and Shawn Richardson

ISBN 0-590-49237-3

12 11 10 9 8 7 6 5 4 3   2 3 4 5/9

Printed in the U.S.A.

Contents

Continued

INTRODUCTION

Welcome to volume two of *Meet the Authors and Illustrators*—a second collection of interviews with 60 very special creators of children's books. A lot of effort went into selecting these talented people. We spoke to a number of teachers and school librarians to find out which authors and illustrators students would most like to read about. Then Deborah Kovacs and James Preller spent many illuminating hours conducting the interviews and, finally, writing the profiles that appear on these pages.

We think you'll be very happy with this collection. In it, you'll find an exciting group of writers and artists—each with a distinct voice and vision. Some make us chuckle, others make us cry, some rely on facts to tell of dramatic events that shaped our history, others spin yarns in irresistible verse. These authors and illustrators bring a rich diversity of experience to their work. They come from near and far: big cities and small towns all over the United States, as well as Puerto Rico, Australia, Canada, Czechoslovakia, China, England, Germany, Holland, and Japan.

And they have great stories to tell. Shonto Begay explains what it's like growing up in a hogan on a Navajo reservation, Bill Martin, Jr. talks about the thrill of becoming a published writer, Faith Ringgold reflects on a wonderful childhood in Harlem, Betty Bao Lord shares the joy and pain of venturing to a new land, and Jerry Spinelli confides how a piece of fried chicken became the inspiration for one of his best-loved books.

We designed this book with your students in mind. When kids learn about their favorite authors and illustrators, they gain valuable insights into the stories they are reading—and the people who created those stories. That means they'll read books by these individuals with greater enthusiasm and understanding. And because each profile is accompanied by a special activity, students' *own* creativity may be sparked, allowing them to join this dynamic community of writers and artists.

We designed this book with you in mind, too. The back of the collection is stocked with great ideas for celebrating your students' favorite authors and illustrators throughout the year. We've even provided an index of their birthdays so you can turn these special occasions into meaningful learning experiences.

We hope you'll like this second volume of *Meet the Authors and Illustrators*. It's certainly been an enriching project for us to work on. We learned a lot about the creative process from the 60 authors and illustrators profiled here, and that learning has helped us reflect on our own craft as editors. In assembling this book, we couldn't help but feel connected to these wonderful personalities. And we have a hunch that you and your students will grow quite attached to them, too.

THE EDITORS

PICTURE BOOKS

AUTHORS AND ILLUSTRATORS

PREFACE

I had my good friend Elana over the other day. She's an elementary teacher in New York City. While we sat in the backyard enjoying the afternoon sun, our meandering conversation turned, as it always turns, to children's books. She told me how much her students loved *Chicka Chicka Boom Boom* by Bill Martin, Jr. and John Archambault. We talked about James Marshall—how sad his death was, what a loss to children's literature—and Elana hilariously described how she used to dress up as Viola Swamp for dramatic readings of *Miss Nelson is Missing!* I asked her if she'd ever read *Chicken Sunday* by Patricia Polacco, or one of my favorites, *Koala Lou* by Mem Fox.

Excited, I told her to wait one minute, rushed into the house, searched through my bookshelves, and came staggering back under a pile of books. I eagerly showed her new favorites by Lane Smith, Barbara Cooney, Gloria Houston, Faith Ringgold, and Shonto Begay. I wanted her to read each book, right there, right then. And more important, I wanted her to love those books—to marvel at the drawings, to laugh at the wit, and, at last, to see how easily she could use these books in her classroom. Of course, Elana saw that part instantly, as all good teachers do.

I suppose this book is my chance to say to a wider audience, "Hey, have you ever checked out Joanne Ryder's books? I think she's great." I hope that you use this second volume of *Meet the Authors and Illustrators* in the classroom—spill coffee on it, leave it out beside the hamster cage, fold back its pages, give it to kids to read and read and read. Each profile has been written not only for teachers, but as a resource for children to enjoy as well. And maybe this book, if it's good enough (and I very much hope it is), will lead to the discovery of many more good books. They sure are out there.

JAMES PRELLER

Shonto Begay

BORN: February 7, 1954, in Shonto, Arizona
HOME: Kayenta, Arizona

SELECTED TITLES

The Mud Pony
1988

Ma'ii and Cousin Horned Toad
1992

◇

A gentle-voiced man, Shonto Begay grew up on a Navajo reservation in the northeast corner of Arizona. The fifth of 16 children born to a Navajo medicine man, Shonto describes living in the earthen hogan (a building usually made of logs and mud): "I grew up with no television, no running water, no electricity," Shonto explains. "The hogan is about 20 feet in diameter, with an earth floor. Everybody sleeps in there. You roll open the sheepskin bedding in the evening. In the morning, after you've slept, you roll it back up. All the living is done in the hogan. If you want privacy you go into the canyons, up to the mesa.

"I grew up tending sheep, staying with the flock all day, riding the horse in the valley, tending the cornfield in the summertime. We all tended the cornfield—it was part of growing up. There were a lot of things to do. By the time you got home in the evening you were really tired so you would just eat and fall asleep. I didn't know there was any other lifestyle outside, beyond the horizons. I thought everybody in the world lived like this. It was normal."

Shonto's father, a well-respected man in the Native American community, made a living through his work as a healer. Shonto's mother, like most Navajo women of the time, was a weaver. Shonto's grandmother and grandfather also played vital roles in everyday family life.

Shonto recalls, "I grew up listening to my grandmother tell coyote stories. With the fire roaring in an old drum stove, shadows flickering in strange dances on the hogan walls, we listened intently as, with animated gestures and disguised voices, she made us laugh."

Shonto believes that these stories are very important. He says, "A lot of our teachings are explained through stories. I think all the Indian stories have messages in them, as opposed to television and other mass-produced forms of entertainment that don't have much redeeming value. Also, stories provide a verbal, historical account of one's identity. As a group of people—a tribe or any other race—stories are one way to preserve a good portion of your culture."

While herding sheep as a child, Shonto would often go to a favorite place he called his "story rock," where he could be alone with his thoughts and dreams. Shonto recalls, "There was one particular place atop the mesa where an outcropping of rock overlooks the whole valley. I could look down into the valley and the only thing I'd hear is the tinkle of sheep bells, the call of the raven somewhere in the distant sky, the wind blowing through the pinyan trees. I would sit there because it was always warmed by the sun in the winter and buffeted by cool air in the summer. I would read my storybooks—folktales, Mark Twain, Jack London."

> ## "Everybody has a culture and an identity that they can draw strength from. Everybody's cultural background is valid and he or she should be proud of it."

⬦

All of his life, Shonto has felt a kinship with nature. He observes, "I grew up in a religion that reveres the earth. Every prayer begins: Mother Earth, Father Sky. The earth is treated just like the mother." The natural world—colorful patterns in the sand, pinyan pines bending in the wind, scattered pieces of driftwood—called out to Shonto as if asking to be drawn. Shonto says, "Looking at nature, one can't help but feel compelled to create."

A DIFFERENT WORLD
Shonto first experienced life outside his own culture when, at the age of four, he went to the Bureau of Indian Affairs boarding school. Shonto learned the English language and discovered such conveniences as electrical lights and modern plumbing. Shonto recalls, "I thought, 'Wow, I didn't know anyone lived like that!' Then I started seeing magazines and realized there was a whole different culture out there. Everything seemed so pretty and convenient and wonderful."

When he was old enough, Shonto set out in an old car to see the world

beyond the horizon. After two years on the road, Shonto ended up in Oakland, California, where he met his wife, Rita. Shonto recalls those days: "I thought, 'This is really great. No more chopping wood, no more hauling water, no more being out in the cold.' It was exciting, but it sort of wore off after a couple of years. Then I longed to get back to my animals, my home. I realized how fortunate I was to have a place to get back to, a place to belong."

After seven years away from his homeland, Shonto returned to begin a new phase in his life. One day, out of the blue, Shonto was contacted by an editor in New York who was looking for a Native American artist to illustrate a Pawnee tale called *The Mud Pony*. Shonto gladly accepted the challenge. His career as a children's book illustrator, and later a writer, had begun.

When you look at Shonto's books, you'll notice that his paintings have a dreamlike quality. Shonto uses an interesting process to create those evocative backgrounds. Salt is the key ingredient. Shonto says, "When I go to schools I do a little demonstration. I put down some very fluid watercolors and then apply salt to them. The salt, of course, draws water to itself and makes nice little effects. That's half of it. Then I have a blow dryer that I use to dry certain parts of the work at various speeds."

When he meets children in schools, Shonto draws upon his own cultural background to make connections. Despite the contrasts, Shonto finds that people share many things in common. "In the end," Shonto has concluded, "we are more alike than different."

THE MUD PONY
Retold by Caron Lee Cohen
Illustrated by Shonto Begay

DO IT YOURSELF!
Shonto offers this advice to children: "Turn the TV off once in a while. Go a day without it. There are so many exciting things that are happening. All it takes is a walk alone, studying and observing nature." Why not try it—go a day without television! Like Shonto Begay, you may find your own story rock, a place to be alone with your thoughts and dreams.

Jan Brett

BORN: December 1, 1949, in Hingham, Massachusetts
HOME: Norwell, Massachusetts

For Jan Brett, drawing and dreaming are almost the same thing. An artist who enjoys peaceful, quiet places, Jan will lose herself in a drawing for hours on end. It is Jan's special time—a time for the imagination, a time for daydreams. The everyday world falls away as she creates a new world, inch by inch, with her detailed illustrations. Jan describes the experience: "I like to put a lot of detail in my work. I work until I feel I've created a world that is possible to walk into. I like to get lost in the place that I'm creating. It's a lot like being in a happy dream."

Jan was a shy child. Uncomfortable with large groups of children, she preferred the company of pencil and paper. She recalls, "I spent hours drawing every day, because that's what I loved to do." Jan also enjoyed reading, especially if it was a book by fellow animal-lover Beatrix Potter. Jan says, "If you had gone to my kindergarten class and asked me what I wanted to be, I'd have said, 'A children's book illustrator.' That's all I've ever wanted to be."

Today Jan is much less shy. But she still feels that she communicates best with her pictures. Thinking of the children who read her books, Jan says, "It's almost like we have a secret language we can share. I love the idea that through my drawings I can communicate with kids. It's like a window we can see each other through." Jan appreciates that children take the extra time to look carefully at her illustrations. She says, "Children will come up to me and say things about my pictures that adults will never notice."

As you can tell from her books, Jan loves animals and nature. "When I was little," Jan says, "I had many pets. We raised guinea pigs and rabbits, and had a donkey and a horse, in addition to the usual dogs and cats. I'll never forget my pet chicken, Delly, who used to ride on my shoulders. Now these animals, along with many others, reappear in my books."

BLENDING IDEAS

Jan's most famous book, *The Wild Christmas Reindeer*, came about in part because of Jan's horse, Westy. But as with most of Jan's book ideas, there wasn't only one source. Her book ideas come from a variety of places. *The Wild Christmas Reindeer* started this way: "I've always imagined what the North Pole would look like. And I thought about it for so long, all of a sudden I thought, this has *got* to be a book!"

Jan wanted the story to be about an

animal. She recalls, "When I started thinking about the North Pole, I couldn't wait to draw the reindeer. I love animals, and I've noticed that if you love your subject, those feelings show in your drawings.

"At the same time I was wondering what could happen to the reindeer, I was having a bothersome time with my horse, Westy. Westy isn't perfect, and I was trying hard to make him obey. I noticed that if I was angry with him and lost my temper, things only got worse. But if I took a deep breath and spoke calmly, he would listen to me."

"Writing a story is like going down a path in the woods. You follow the path. You don't worry about getting lost, you just go."

Jan decided that her story would be about an elf who has to get Santa's reindeer ready for the long Christmas ride. She sketched out a rough version, or dummy, of the book. Those rough pictures, drawn in about two weeks, showed what was going to happen on each page. Then came the more challenging part—the six-month-long process of finishing the illustrations.

But in order to complete the drawings, Jan had to find a model for Teeka, the elf in the story. Using real models, Jan believes, keeps her drawings fresh and makes the character seem more believable to the reader.

Finding a model is never easy. Jan says it's like looking for a needle in a haystack. And in this case, it was particularly difficult. After all, where was Jan going to find an elf?

Eventually, Jan settled on a shy girl named Natalie. Jan recalls, "One day

my husband came home and said, 'Oh, I met a little girl who looks like an elf.' That's all he said. When I met her, she was one of those children who didn't talk at all to people, but when she saw an animal she lit up."

Imagine that you were going to be a model for one of Jan's stories. First you'd go shopping with Jan because you'd need to wear the right clothes. Then you'd sit down with Jan and read the dummy version of the book together. You'd talk about how the character feels and maybe give Jan an idea or two. Then you'd act out the entire book: leaping, walking, sitting— doing everything the character might do. All the while, Jan would watch very closely and take lots of photographs.

When illustrating, Jan doesn't try to copy the photographs, though. "I'll take them out and glance at them," she says, "but I'll put them away. I'm afraid if I copy from the photograph, the illustration will look stiff and frozen."

As a child, Jan often felt frustrated by book illustrations that didn't give enough information. That's why she likes to put in all the little details. Jan often uses borders to get all her ideas into the book. She explains, "I draw borders when I have too many ideas. In *The Mitten*, the borders show Nicki trekking through the woods and scaring different animals out of their hiding places. When you turn a page in the book, you can see the animal that comes next."

DO IT YOURSELF!

Here's something fun to do. But first, listen to Jan Brett: "Everyone likes to draw what they love or do the best. For example, the hedgehog is my favorite animal and I think you can tell—it comes out better than an animal I don't like as much." Now it's your turn. Draw a picture of something you love or know about. Like Jan Brett, you might find it helpful to take a closer look at the real thing before you start your drawing.

Marc Brown

BORN: November 25, 1946, in Erie, Pennsylvania
HOME: Hingham, Massachusetts

SELECTED TITLES

Arthur's Nose
1976

Arthur's Eyes
1979

The True Francine
1981

The Bionic Bunny Show
1984

Hand Rhymes
1985

Dinosaurs Divorce
1986

Arthur's Baby
1987

Arthur's Birthday
1989

Visiting the Art Museum
1990

Arthur Meets the President
1991

Arthur's New Puppy
1993

Need a new idea? Try looking around. That's what Marc Brown does. "There are wonderful ideas for stories all around," says Marc. "All you have to do is keep your eyes and your ears open. It might be something that happens at home with your sister. It might happen in your classroom. It might be on the bus. I feel envious of kids, because they are right in the middle of it, while I have to try and remember!"

Whenever Marc has time, he loves to visit children in schools. For him, it is a way to connect with his readers. It helps Marc remember his own days in school. During these visits, he often finds material he can use in his own writing. "After all," Marc admits, "practically all of my characters come from third grade."

When Marc steps into a school, he is all eyes and ears. "I go into overdrive," he says. "I find the day so exciting and intense. I'm like a sponge. There's all this great material everywhere. I try to remember it all." A passing conversation, the way a child opens a lunch box in the cafeteria—any of these ordinary details might spark an idea for Marc's next book.

When Marc gets an idea—it can be a picture, a funny ending to a story, the name of a character, even a book title—he stores it away until the time is right for that idea to "grow up" to become a book. Sometimes it takes years. "Sometimes," Marc confesses, "those ideas never grow up." He explains, "My ideas have to germinate a long time before they come together in a book. I depend on drawers full of scraps of stories, bits of dialogue, quick drawings, titles, concepts. At any one time there are probably 100 ideas in the drawer, not all of them good. Sometimes just one small part of a drawing, one line of a vignette is usable."

CREATING ARTHUR

Marc Brown is most famous for creating the character of Arthur. Arthur was born when Marc began telling bedtime stories to his son, Tolon. Marc remembers, "Most of the stories were about animals. One night our story was about an aardvark who hated his nose. The aardvark, of course, was Arthur. That bedtime story became *Arthur's Nose*, the first book in the Arthur adventure series."

It's not easy coming up with new story ideas for Arthur, but Marc gets plenty of help from students and teachers. "*Arthur Meets the President* was suggested by a teacher," Marc says. "As soon as she said it—that

Arthur should visit the White House—three separate ideas came together. I'd always wanted to do a book on the White House. I'd also wanted to do a book about a field trip. And I'd wanted to do one about Arthur winning a contest. I just didn't know how to do it. Suddenly all those half-formed ideas came together."

MARC BROWN
ARTHUR MEETS THE PRESIDENT
AN ARTHUR ADVENTURE

> ### "I am thrilled by children's reactions to my books. That's what fuels me to write other books."

Marc studied to be a painter in school. Maybe that's why he thinks that writing is a lot more difficult than drawing. "The writing is the hardest part," Marc admits. "It's something I *have* to do in order to get to the part I like." He adds with a laugh, "I wish someone else would do it for me, so I could just draw the pictures and have fun!"

Difficult or not, Marc realizes that writing gives him a chance to explore his own feelings. "When I wrote *Arthur's Eyes*, I was going through a divorce. The story happened to be about an aardvark getting glasses, but when I finished I realized it was really about adjusting to a whole new life. It was about trying something new, getting used to new things. It was about me."

Marc offers, "The book I'm proudest of is *Dinosaurs Divorce*. When I was first divorced, my two sons stayed with me. But all the books in the library showed the kids living with their mom. The dads would all go off to a hotel. My kids wondered what was wrong with *our* divorce." Working with his second wife, Laurene, Marc set out to write a book that would give children practical information about divorce. He says, "Every family divorces differently. Some ways, of course, are better than others, but there's no one right way."

Marc often discusses *Dinosaurs Divorce* when he visits classrooms. He says, "Afterwards, kids who are going through a divorce come up to me. They just *have* to talk about it." That's when Marc Brown knows that he has done something good—something meaningful—with his art. He wants *Dinosaurs Divorce* to serve as a starting point for important discussions. Marc feels it's important for children to express their feelings. He says, with a hint of frustration in his voice, "We are so bad at letting people talk about their feelings. We are so afraid. What's wrong with us? They are just feelings—and they can hurt you if you don't talk about them."

As a child, Marc spent a lot of time alone, living in what he calls a fantasy world. Oddly enough, his love for stories did not come from books. He recalls, "I don't remember many books as a child. But I spent weekends with my grandmother and great-grandmother, and they were wonderful storytellers. That's where I really became fond of stories—and it was my job to supply the pictures."

DO IT YOURSELF!

Imagine that you are Marc Brown. It's your job to come up with an interesting story about Arthur. Remember, Marc has already written 18 Arthur books, so it won't be easy thinking up something exciting and new. When you've finished your story, you might want to send it with a letter to Marc.

Barbara Cooney

BORN: August 6, 1917, in Brooklyn, New York
HOME: Damariscotta, Maine

SELECTED TITLES

Chanticleer and the Fox
(Caldecott Medal)
1958

Seven Little Rabbits
1972

Ox-Cart Man
(Caldecott Medal)
1979

Miss Rumphius
1982

The Story of Holly and Ivy
1985

Island Boy
1988

The Year of the Perfect Christmas Tree
1988

Hattie and the Wild Waves
1990

Roxaboxen
1991

Emily
1992

Letting Swift River Go
1992

It is snowing in Damariscotta, Maine. A foot has fallen since the previous night and now a soft white blanket covers Barbara Cooney's world. "It's wonderful," Barbara says as she looks up at the four skylights of her attic studio. "It's lovely to sit here and watch the weather come down." Barbara has already taken a long morning walk in the snow and now she's ready to talk about her work.

"Of all the books I have done," Barbara says, "*Miss Rumphius, Island Boy,* and *Hattie and the Wild Waves* are closest to my heart. They are as near as I ever will come to an autobiography."

Barbara Cooney published her first book in 1940, more than 50 years ago. Though she has won two Caldecott Medals (*Chanticleer and the Fox,* 1959; *Ox-Cart Man,* 1981), she says she is proudest of the work that came *after* those books were published— after Barbara reached an age, in fact, when most people quit work and retire. Barbara tells us, "I knew I had to change after *Ox-Cart Man.* I mean, how many medals do you need to make you feel that you've finished your apprenticeship?" She adds with confidence: "I think I've done my best work in the last 10 years, starting with *Miss Rumphius.*"

Stitching together pieces from her own life—and the life of her family— Barbara wrote a story about a young girl named Alice Rumphius who was determined to accomplish three things when she grew up: she would visit faraway places, she would live by the sea, and she would do something to make the world more beautiful.

Barbara explains, "I was trying to make a modern fairy tale, but it happened that people really latched on to the message. Children write letters to me about what they are going to do to make the world better." But, Barbara is quick to say, "I wasn't trying to preach at all—I would *never* do that. Basically I took episodes from my life and made a story."

BLENDING FACT WITH FICTION

Near her home in Maine, Barbara had heard a story about a woman called the Lupine Lady. "She lived in this area and used to go around throwing lupine seeds all over the place. She gets a lot of credit for these wild fields of lupine around here. I thought, well, that's a nice thing to peg a story on, but I didn't know how to do it. Then one day I sat down and embellished the idea with memories of my mother, my grandmother, my great-grandfather, and my travels."

Barbara points out that Miss

Rumphius isn't Barbara—although she used a lot of her own experiences to create the character. She offers examples: "Little Alice has a grandfather who carves cigar-store Indians. I had a great-grandfather who also made cigar-store Indians. My grandmother actually did help him put the skies in his paintings. I was never a librarian, but I did live across the street from a nice old library in a Massachusetts town where my husband was a doctor. The greenhouse is at Smith College, where I went to school."

Like Miss Rumphius, Barbara enjoyed many adventures while traveling. She relates, "I've done lots and lots of traveling to all sorts of exotic places. Really, that book would have been twice as long if my editor had let me put in all the places I wanted to draw and write about!"

After the success of *Miss Rumphius,* Barbara went on to illustrate more books by other authors. But she soon returned to a subject close to her heart. "*Island Boy* is my hymn to Maine," she confides.

Last in Barbara's trilogy is *Hattie and the Wild Waves,* the story of a young girl who follows her dream to become an artist. While the facts of the story are based upon her mother's life, Barbara confesses: "I think Hattie is probably me."

Barbara hints that she may write more autobiographical books in the future, yet she won't talk about them. "I'm hoping it will be a quintet, but I haven't gotten that far yet," she says. "You lose your energy to write if you talk about things that are clicking in your mind. So I don't." But, she adds with a light laugh, "I *do* have a couple of ideas floating around."

Barbara is acclaimed for doing thorough research. She will do nearly anything to make sure her illustrations are honest and authentic. When she was illustrating *Chanticleer and the Fox,* Barbara borrowed chickens from a neighbor. For *The Story of Holly and Ivy,* she visited England's Scotland Yard to find out how many buttons a policeman has on his uniform! And for *The Year of the Perfect Christmas Tree,* Barbara spent a week in the Appalachian mountains— climbing hills, visiting homes, getting props, observing how the setting sun lights the valley. It was a lot simpler to research *Ox-Cart Man.* Barbara says with a laugh, "All I had to do was step outside my back door!"

Once an avid photographer, Barbara still uses a camera for her research. She says taking pictures has taught her an important lesson: "When you are doing photography," she explains, "you are painting with light. Photography taught me to think about light in a new way. I think that there's a sense of atmosphere in my pictures now that wasn't there in my earlier books."

How does Barbara Cooney describe what drives her to write? "I think what I'm doing is trying to communicate the things I love in the world, to make a record of what captivates me. With each photograph or drawing I say, 'Isn't this great? Isn't this delicious? Isn't this funny?'"

Hattie and the Wild Waves
Story and Pictures by BARBARA COONEY
SCHOLASTIC

"Sometimes you look at your work on the drawing board, and it's like a battlefield. You are fighting to get the picture to turn out right."

DO IT YOURSELF!

Read *Miss Rumphius.* Like Alice, think about what you might do to make the world a better place. Then do it! You might like to write about what you've done—and why.

Lulu Delacre

BORN: December 20, 1957, in Puerto Rico
HOME: Silver Springs, Maryland

SELECTED TITLES

Nathan and Nicholas Alexander
1986

Nathan's Fishing Trip
1988

Arroz Con Leche: Popular Songs and Rhymes from Latin America
1989

Time for School, Nathan!
1989

Las Navidades: Popular Christmas Songs from Latin America
1990

Nathan's Balloon Adventure
1991

Vejigantes Masquerade
1993

———◇———

ulu Delacre (pronounced De-LAK-ray) recently visited Miami, Florida. She walked the streets, sampled Cuban dishes, talked to many people, and took *lots* of pictures. Sounds like a nice vacation, doesn't it? But Lulu wasn't on vacation—she was doing research for her next book.

"Research is a lot of fun," says Lulu. "That's when you learn. You get to talk to people, you get to see places, you get to take pictures and read wonderful books!"

Lulu travels great distances to visit the places she plans to feature in her books. While staying in these far-off cities, Lulu notices the clothes the people wear, the games they play, and the way a certain street looks in the sun-drenched afternoon light. Lulu feels it's very important for each of her illustrations to be accurate. For with these details, Lulu hopes to convey the subtle flavors of everyday life.

Lulu began her writing career with *Nathan and Nicholas Alexander*, a story about a gentle elephant who befriends a rather haughty mouse. Lulu, a wife and mother of two daughters, says, "Nathan is the son I never had." In all, Lulu has created four books featuring these two unlikely friends.

Though Lulu has enjoyed the Nathan series, Lulu's more recent bilingual books hold a special place in her heart. Perhaps that's because these books (*Arroz Con Leche, Las Navidades, Vejigantes Masquerade*) are more connected to her own childhood.

Lulu explains, "Writing bilingual books has been the greatest challenge of my career. It's a big task, dealing with two languages—one of them my mother tongue—and portraying my own culture with authenticity in both words and pictures. It's also an important duty of which I feel very proud."

CELEBRATING HER CULTURE

From early childhood, Lulu has moved easily from one culture to another. She's had to: Her parents are from Argentina; she was born and raised in Puerto Rico; she studied art in France; and she now lives in Maryland! Of course, given these biographical facts, it is only natural for Lulu to say, "I love to see it when different cultures come together."

But when Lulu went to the library to find books for her own two daughters to read, she realized how hard it was to find children's books that represented her own Latin

American culture. Lulu knew how to solve that problem, though—she'd write the books herself!

Lulu, who taught her two daughters to read in Spanish, continues, "I thought there had to be parents like me, who had children unfamiliar with their heritage. Many children, in order to integrate, try to forget their backgrounds. They don't learn their parents' language and folklore. I felt there was a need for a book that would provide a sample of my folklore and a positive image of the Latin American people."

> **"Everybody has something to say, something that is close to his or her heart. It's a matter of being courageous enough to put the thoughts and feelings into words."**

Lulu hopes that children will value their families' traditions as well as the traditions of other cultures. It doesn't matter if they are Italian or Irish, Chinese or Puerto Rican. Lulu also stresses the importance of learning about others. "The more you know about another person's cultural heritage, the more you can understand why they act certain ways. When you learn to appreciate other people's cultural and ethnic backgrounds, a positive energy develops that may lead to harmony. I believe this sharing should happen in all directions, between all people."

Lulu Delacre dreams of a day when classrooms are full of children of different backgrounds who appreciate each other's differences. Lulu states, "We need to achieve that among all cultures—*without forgetting our roots.* We should celebrate the differences that make us unique."

Lulu enjoys visiting schools and working with children. She tells this story: "Last year I conducted a picture book workshop where I took 75 second-graders through the process of creating a children's book. I told them, 'You have to start with an idea. Well,' I ask, 'where do ideas come from? Why don't you write about something that you've lived, that you've done—a day that was very sad, a day that was wonderful and happy. *Write about something that has happened to you.*'"

The author concludes: "It's much better to write about something you know than about something you don't know."

DO IT YOURSELF!

Lulu created two bilingual books by researching the songs she knew as a child. Why not try a similar project? Ask an older person—a teacher, a parent, a grandparent—to sing a song he or she knew as a child. Carefully write down all the words. Then, like Lulu, draw a picture that captures the spirit of the song!

Lois Ehlert

BORN: November 9, 1934, in Beaver Dam, Wisconsin
HOME: Milwaukee, Wisconsin

SELECTED TITLES

Growing Vegetable Soup
1987

Planting a Rainbow
1988

Chicka Chicka Boom Boom
1989

Color Zoo
(Caldecott Honor Book)
1989

Eating the Alphabet
1989

Feathers for Lunch
1990

Fish Eyes: A Book You Can Count On
1990

Red Leaf, Yellow Leaf
1991

Circus
1992

Lois Ehlert had been having a tough time. No matter how hard she tried, she could not come up with an idea for her next book. How did she solve her problem? By *not* trying at all!

Lois tells this story: "I'd been trying to find a new idea for a book. Everything I tried just looked really dumb. Most times I do both the writing and the art, so I don't have anyone to help with the ideas. One Saturday I finally gave up and took a train to Chicago for the day. I spent the whole day in the Art Institute of Chicago. I had a great time. Then a few days later, while I was eating my breakfast, my idea came into focus. I wrote the words down as fast as I could, finished eating, and then wrote for the rest of the day. I may throw all of it away; it's certainly not in good shape yet. But somewhere in it, I believe there is a little beginning of a book. If I get lucky, maybe you will see it in a book in about two or three years."

That's the creative process in a nutshell—a complete and total mystery! And though Lois does not know where her ideas come from, she does offer this insight: "I think I was born with certain ideas and feelings just waiting to burst out."

She believes that all the hard work, the endless research, and the anxiety-filled hours of *trying* to have an idea help the process along. "But," Lois adds, "the truth is that you never know when an idea will come to you."

GROWING UP CREATIVE... NATURALLY!

Colorful, bright, bold, stunning—these are some of the words that describe Lois's artwork. One book reviewer even called it "eye-zapping!" Whatever words we find to describe Lois's books, each page shows the handiwork of a true artist.

"I just love color," Lois affirms. "It makes me happy!" It's true: There is a joyfulness to her books—a sense of wonder, playfulness, startling beauty. A lover of long walks and open spaces, Lois strives to connect her readers to the natural world of gardens and trees, flowers and animals. Lois admits, "I'm trying to use my art to teach a little, making children a little more appreciative of the flowers they can see, or helping to open up their eyes to the beautiful birds flying overhead."

"I guess everyone is influenced by their own experiences," Lois says. "Being creative was most natural to me as I was growing up. My mother sewed and my dad built things out of wood. Dad had a workshop in the basement, Mom had a room with all of her material, thread, patterns, and sewing machine. I got good scraps from both of them. They didn't think it was unusual for me to be making things because that's what they did."

In a house where everybody was busy making things, it was predictable that Lois would create art of her own. As a child, Lois also loved going to the library with her younger brother and sister. It was a joyous time. "We would go to the library once a week. The maximum number of books we could take out was five per person. We ended up with 15 books each week. We'd take those home, and the three of us would read all 15 one way or another. We'd take them back and next week get 15 new ones!"

She went on to art school, which she enjoyed very much. Lois discovered that she didn't like drawing as much as she liked cutting and pasting. She describes the thinking behind this preference: "Unless I used a lot of erasers and kept changing the drawing, it never was exactly the way I wanted it. For instance, if I drew a face, I would never know whether the mouth would look better one inch closer to the nose unless I did the drawing over and over again. But if I cut out a mouth of paper, I could try it in different positions until I found the best one, then glue it down permanently."

This art technique, called collage, gave Lois the flexibility she sought. She delights in making pictures out of "found" materials—scraps of paper, pieces of fabric, and so on. What's more, it connects Lois to her own childhood days, using materials that her parents left behind.

"I'm just like my Dad," Lois admits. "I save all sorts of things— scraps of leather, shiny buttons, colored ribbons, telephone wire. All of this stuff is stored in an old wooden seed box, waiting for a place in my artwork."

Most times Lois writes and illustrates her books. But when an editor sends her a manuscript written by someone else, Lois will sometimes agree to provide illustrations. One day Lois received a manuscript by Bill Martin, Jr. called *Chicka Chicka Boom Boom*. She almost turned it down!

Lois recalls, "The first time I read it, I thought, 'This is one I'm not going to be able to do. There's no way—I'll just have to send this back to the editor.' Then I started thinking about it, reading the text over again—it has such a nice rhythm. I got to thinking about it almost as a piece of music. I thought, 'Well, I can maybe just sort of make it like a fiesta.'"

Lois went to work: cutting, pasting, painting. Slowly, her ideas started to take shape. Lois recalls the process: "I added the borders on the outside and started cutting paper and seeing how I could *possibly* get a letter of the alphabet to climb up a coconut tree."

> **"I derive so much pleasure in looking. I hope children will too."**

DO IT YOURSELF!

Lois Ehlert believes that every artist needs his or her own space—a special place where he or she can be left alone to create. She offers this advice: "Find a spot where you live—it can be small—to keep all the supplies you might need when you write or draw. When an idea comes, you'll be ready. Good luck to you. I know I can always use a bit of luck myself!"

Mem Fox

BORN: March 5, 1946, in Melbourne, Australia
HOME: Adelaide, Australia

SELECTED TITLES

Possum Magic
1983

Wilfrid Gordon McDonald Partridge
1984

Hattie and the Fox
1986

Koala Lou
1987

Guess What?
1988

With Love at Christmas
1988

Night Noises
1989

Shoes from Grandpa
1989

Dear Mem Fox, I Have Read All Your Books Even the Pathetic Ones
1992

Mem Fox is a woman of great enthusiasms. When talking, Mem will often hoot with delight and flail her arms to make a point. Or she'll lean forward, listening intently, her eyes fixed and steady. And always, at a moment's notice, Mem is ready to fill a room with uproarious laughter.

Quite naturally, this emotional zest spills over into Mem's writing. And she's glad it does. In fact, Mem believes that, above all, a book should make the reader *feel*. "Emotion is to picture books as flour is to bread," Mem contends. "If we don't laugh, gasp, block our ears, sigh, vomit, giggle, curl our toes, sympathize, feel pain, weep, or shiver during the reading of a picture book, then surely the writer has wasted our time, our money, and our precious trees."

Born in Melbourne, Australia, Mem moved to Africa with her parents, who were missionaries, when she was only six months old. They lived in Rhodesia, now called Zimbabwe. Mem loved her first school and made many friends. She recalls, "I spoke the local language, Ndebele, better than I spoke English. Like the other children in my class, I learned to write by writing letters with my finger, in the dusty, red earth."

Growing up in an all-black community, Mem never saw herself as different. "Until I was five or so," Mem says, "I believed I was black. I was the only white child at the mission school, blind to my own whiteness and absolutely astonished when the local authorities told my parents I would be required to attend a school for white children. I clearly remember thinking, 'Gee, I must be special if I have to go to a white school.' It really didn't occur to me that I was white."

GETTING PUBLISHED...FINALLY!
While growing up, Mem made occasional stabs at writing. Laughing at the recollection, she confides that her first book, written at age 10, "was about the thrilling subject of soil erosion." However, the world of theater also tugged at Mem's heart. At age 19, Mem moved to London to study drama, but after a few years decided that she preferred writing to acting. Back in Australia, now with a husband, Malcolm, and a child, Chloe, Mem began to work on a story called *Hush, the Invisible Mouse*. Mem remembers the motivation behind writing the story: "It came about because I was enraged that my daughter had no books to help her identify herself as an Australian, to

help her feel proud of her country and heritage." So Mem wrote the story of *Hush*, and lovingly wrapped it in the texture and details of Australian life.

Mem tried to get her picture book published. She tried...and tried...and tried. But no one seemed interested in her story. Mem recalls those difficult days: "Each time I received a rejection slip I felt ashamed that I'd dared to believe the book might be worth publishing."

"I read a lot, which helps me to know how to write as well as what to write about. My best advice for anyone who would like to be a writer is: Read!!!"

◇

But, with the unfailing support of her husband, Mem persevered. She rewrote her story 23 times. Finally, one quiet day in Australia, the air was pierced with Mem's whoops of joy. After five years and nine rejections, a publisher wanted to publish her book. "I was wild with excitement," Mem remembers. "I changed the mouse to a possum and called the story *Possum Magic*. The irony," Mem adds with obvious satisfaction, "is that *Possum Magic* became the best-selling children's book in the history of Australia."

Of all the books she has written, Mem's favorite is *Koala Lou*. This may be because the central character in the story—an earnest little koala who desperately wants to succeed and be loved—is really Mem. Mem explains, "*Koala Lou* is about me and my mum, who's really tough. She is a female Tarzan, the kind of person who will kill a snake with a crowbar without flinching. She loves me a lot but she

never says 'I love you.' Never."

When writing, Mem needs solitude, silence, and a clean work space. Getting the initial idea is the first and hardest part (though, Mem would say, there are *many* hard parts). Mem explains, "I always write in pencil first so that I can rub out as I go. My early drafts are incredibly messy. I type my later drafts on a word-processor." Because she still holds a job as a teacher (which she loves), Mem squeezes her writing into whatever time is left over—usually late at night, on weekends, and on vacations.

"The ideas leap into my head from real life, and if they don't, I don't write," she confides. "I'm not one of those disciplined writers who sits down at a blank piece of paper or a blank computer screen and says, 'I'm not moving until I've written 500 words.' I could sit there for a *month* without writing a word."

A fierce perfectionist, Mem actually spends most of her "writing time" rewriting. She provides an example: "It took me two years to write *Koala Lou*, even though it's only 410 words. I did 49 drafts for *Koala Lou* before the book was ready to be published."

Mem believes that revision is a very important part of writing. She says, "Picture books are so short that it's essential that the best words be placed in the best possible order." Mem will spend an entire day agonizing over a single sentence. In a silent room, Mem will read the sentence aloud to herself, rewrite it, then read it aloud again. For Mem, the process can be worse than hard work. She cries, "It's torture!"

KOALA LOU

WRITTEN BY **Mem Fox**   ILLUSTRATED BY **Pamela Lofts**

DO IT YOURSELF!

Mem's books are loaded with action and good dialogue. She strives to reveal characters by what they do and say, rather than by describing them. That's why it's fun to put on a play based on her books. *Wilfrid Gordon McDonald Partridge* is a great place to start, but use any book you like. You'll have to get some classmates to help out. On with the show!

Gail Gibbons

BORN: August 1, 1944, in Oak Park, Illinois
HOME: Corinth, Vermont

SELECTED TITLES

*The Seasons
of Arnold's
Apple Tree*
1984

*Check It Out!:
The Book About
Libraries*
1985

The Milk Makers
1985

*From Path to
Highway:
The Story of the
Boston Post Road*
1986

Trains
1987

Monarch Butterfly
1989

*How a House
Is Built*
1990

*Weather Words and
What They Mean*
1990

*Surrounded By
Sea: Life on a
New England
Fishing Island*
1991

Spiders
1993

A strong-willed, independent child, Gail Gibbons used to drive adults a little crazy. "I drove my parents nuts," she admits with a laugh. "And I drove my teachers nuts, too, because I wouldn't fit into their ideas of what kids were *supposed* to do. I was usually in the last seat in the row, because the teacher couldn't see what I was doing back there. I wanted to be drawing and sketching and doing other things."

Gail wasn't the kind of child who settled for a simple answer, either. Even as a child, she had a thirst to understand things. It was never enough for Gail to know what time it was, she had to know how the whole clock worked! That's probably why Gail writes nonfiction books today. She thinks the world is full of all sorts of neat, interesting stuff. Gail loves learning new things and explaining them with words and pictures to young readers.

Gail began her career by working in television. She used to work as a graphic artist on *The Today Show*, *Saturday Night Live*, and a children's show, *Take a Giant Step*. Gail remembers, "That's when the interest in children's books began...so I started writing and illustrating for children."

Encouraged by her husband, Kent, Gail decided to try her hand at nonfiction books. At that time, most nonfiction books were drab and dull. Almost none had colorful illustrations. Gail felt that she could use the techniques she had learned in television graphics to make nonfiction books that were bright and alive. Gail explains, "With television graphics, you are lucky if the piece you design is on the screen for six seconds. So I had learned how to make art that's simplified and easily readable. It has to be something that grabs you—not cluttered and fancy. When I'm doing a book, it's pretty much the same thing. I love working with bright, bold, beautiful colors."

FROM THE BEGINNING

Now the author of more than 50 books for children, Gail begins each book by selecting a topic, usually with the help of an editor. It's important that they both agree. Gail says, "This morning an editor called and asked if I wanted to do a couple of sports books. Well I don't like sports, so I don't want to do that. It has to be something that I'm interested in." Once they agree on a topic, Gail moves on to the next stage: research.

"I go to bookstores and libraries to gather information, but I don't trust books solely, because they can have mistakes. So I find an expert, someone who knows a lot about the subject I'm writing about. That way I'm sure to get the most up-to-date information.

"I over-research," Gail admits. "I always end up with much more information than I can use. I want to make absolutely sure I've covered everything. If you notice, in a lot of my books there's a lot of information on page 32. Those are extra things that I found that I think are sort of neat, except I couldn't fit them elsewhere in the book."

> ## "I like to come away from reading a book with the feeling that I've learned something. That's why I like nonfiction."

Then comes perhaps the most important stage of all. Gail begins the painstaking process of selecting the most important facts and organizing them into a clear structure. In an approach similar to the way she draws pictures, Gail tries to simplify the information, deciding which details are essential and which details only make it more complicated. Gail is always asking herself, "What's the most important thing?"

Like many writers, Gail finds that revision is difficult. "It can really be draining at times," she admits. "Like when you are explaining how a skyscraper is built and you only have 27 pages, three sentences per page. It's really a challenge. So I overwrite at first. Then I start chopping away. I start slimming it down." Gail will rewrite a book about five or six times before she's finally happy with it.

Gail enjoys the challenge of her work. She says, "I have a real love for nonfiction writing. To me, putting a nonfiction book together is like watching the pieces of a puzzle finally fitting together. Bit by bit it takes its form."

A mother of two children, Becky and Eric, Gail believes it's important to keep in touch with her readers. She travels about seven weeks a year, going from classroom to classroom. "I love it!" Gail says enthusiastically. "I really like to see how kids react to what I do. I like their input. A lot of times I get ideas from them."

Letters from readers also help Gail find out what children really think about her books. She describes her most memorable letter: "The best letter I ever got went like this: 'Dear Gail, I love your books. Right now I am—oh there's a spider crawling across the page! SQUASH.'" Gail laughs and says, "There was a dead spider squashed right on the letter. It was hysterical. I saved that letter. And I still have the dead spider!"

Speaking of spiders, Gail recently finished a book called *Spiders*. Gail says, "I sure wouldn't do a book on spiders in a cute way. If I'm talking about spiders, why not show them for what they are? Spiders aren't cute." Gail states with conviction, "The real thing is interesting enough on its own."

DO IT YOURSELF!

Like Gail Gibbons, select a topic to write about. Then go to the library and begin your research. You may want to find an expert to help you. Decide which facts are most fun and important. And remember Gail's tip: "Write about something you know about. Write about what you like. You'll enjoy it a lot more!"

Patricia Reilly Giff

BORN: April 26, 1935, in Brooklyn, New York
HOME: Weston, Connecticut

SELECTED TITLES

Fourth Grade Celebrity
1979

The Girl Who Knew It All
1979

Today Was a Terrible Day
1980

Have You Seen Hyacinth Macaw?
1981

The Winter Worm Business
1981

Gift of the Pirate Queen
1982

The Almost Awful Play
1983

The Kids of the Polk Street School series
1985–

Watch Out, Ronald Morgan!
1985

Ronald Morgan Goes to Bat
1988

The Lincoln Lions Band series
1992–

"**A**nybody can write a book," states Patricia Reilly Giff. "I mean, look at me. Over 60 books and not one bit of talent.

"I know it sounds funny, but I really do believe it. Writing is something you have to learn. It is a craft. It takes practice. If you set your mind to something, no matter how hard it is, you can do it. That's my message to kids: *Go for it*. If you want something in life, work at it and you can get it."

Patricia (Pat to her friends) sees herself as living proof that an ordinary person can become a successful writer. She stresses, "I don't think writing is a gift. We learn to speak, we learn to read, we learn to write. Writing is a natural thing, not a special talent. Look at sports. When you see a great baseball pitcher on television, don't think it's just talent. That pitcher was probably throwing baseballs to his father when he was two years old. Writing is something you learn, because you do it all the time."

A LATE BLOOMER

Pat's career did not come easy. Ever since she was a child, Pat wanted to be a writer. But as she grew older, she became nervous about sharing her work with others. Pat confesses, "I didn't write until I was grown up because I didn't think I was good enough. I was afraid people might laugh at me."

It wasn't until she was 40 that Pat made a brave decision. She would write a story—even, she says, if it took

the rest of her life. "I decided that I would write every day for a year," Pat explains. Working full-time as a teacher, Pat would drag herself out of bed in the early morning to write for an hour. Pat recalls, "Slowly and painfully, I began to form the words, the sentences. And then suddenly, writing became one of the most important parts of my life, a part that now I couldn't do without."

Today, Patricia Reilly Giff is praised as a writer who truly understands children. When she writes dialogue, it crackles with energy. When she describes a classroom scene, it springs vividly to life. And it should—Pat has spent plenty of time in schools, first as a classroom teacher and then as a reading specialist.

Pat says, "I wanted to write about kids. I wanted to write about *their* world. The cafeteria, what goes on during holidays, climbing the ropes in gym—all those things had happened again and again in my life. After I started working on the *Polk Street* series, school life really began to come alive in my writing."

Pat draws upon real people as a basis for her characters. She thinks of the kids she knew in school, her own three children, and the feelings she herself had as a child. For instance, the character of Ronald Morgan is based upon a former student of hers. "Oh, he was a desperado. He was unbelievable. He used to say to me, 'If you tie me to the table, I'll learn to read.' But," she warmly recalls, "he was *so* cute."

Pat identifies with the underdog, the kid who isn't perfect. She likes kids who don't always hit home runs, who don't always get 100s on tests. Pat advises, "You never want to write about a perfect person. Look at Ramona Quimby. She's not perfect—but it's the failings that remind us of ourselves. That's what builds a character."

Here's how Pat begins a book: "I think of three things. First of all, a person. I think of a zippy kid. I lie in the middle of the living room rug, I shut my eyes, and I try to think about somebody who is funny, and quick, and lively. So that's the first step—envisioning the character. Then I drop that person into a place where I've been, someplace I know really well, so I don't get mixed up. Then I give that person a problem. And that's all I know. When I start the first page, I don't know anything that's going to happen to that kid. Then I almost watch it happen. I close my eyes, and see what's happening. That's how the book gets written."

Pat loves to listen to kids talk. It helps her write dialogue. "Writing dialogue is my strength," she says. "I almost hate to say that, because serious readers may not think it's important. But for me, dialogue is the most wonderful part of writing. I can remember exact conversations from 25 years ago. I can remember the *sound*

of a person's voice."

Throughout Pat's life, from childhood to adulthood, at work and at play, books have always been close by. Cherished objects, they have played a central role in her world. Pat remembers, "As a child, I read in bed before the sun was up, then hunched over the breakfast table with a book in my lap. After school I'd sit in the kitchen, leaning against the warm radiator, dreaming over a story. My mother would say, 'Go out and play, go out and play.' I hated to go out and play! All I wanted to do was dream over stories."

Years later, nothing much has changed. Wherever Pat goes, there's sure to be a book within easy reach. In fact, Pat loves books so much, she recently realized a lifelong dream. Today she owns a children's bookstore in Fairfield, Connecticut, with her husband, three children, and two daughters-in-law. "It's called 'The Dinosaur's Paw' after one of my books," Pat says. "Running a bookstore is hard, hard work—but we love it."

What's the best part? "That's easy!" Pat exclaims. "We get to read all those great books!"

A YEARLING BOOK

A Polk Street Special

Write Up a Storm with the Polk Street School

Patricia Reilly Giff

Includes a special insert you can make into your own book!

Illustrated by Blanche Sims

DO IT YOURSELF!

How do people talk? If you are writing dialogue, it's an important question. Patricia Reilly Giff listens carefully when people speak. She has noticed, for example, that people rarely finish their sentences. Think of two people you know very well—two friends, perhaps—and write down a conversation they might have. Try to make it as realistic as possible!

Paul Goble

BORN: September 27, 1933, in Haslemere, England
HOME: Lincoln, Nebraska

SELECTED TITLES

The Girl Who Loved Wild Horses
(Caldecott Medal)
1978

The Gift of the Sacred Dog
1980

Star Boy
1980

Buffalo Woman
1984

The Great Race of the Birds and Animals
1985

Death of the Iron Horse
1987

Her Seven Brothers
1988

Iktomi and the Boulder
1988

Dream Wolf
1990

I Sing for the Animals
1991

Crow Chief: A Plains Indian Story
1992

Love Flute
1992

Paul Goble has been interested in Native American culture for as long as he can remember. He recalls, "One of my early memories is of walking around my suburban neighborhood in England, dressed in my American Indian regalia: fringed shirt, leggings, and war bonnet, all of which my mother had made for me. I remember being absolutely certain that anyone who saw me would think I was a real Indian!"

As a child, Paul longed to visit the land where Native Americans once flourished. When he was 26 years old, Paul finally came to America and witnessed Native American dances and ceremonies. Though exhilarating, the experience left him saddened. Paul saw that many of the Indian children were more interested in baseball than in their own heritage. It gave Paul a reason to write. He says, "It was primarily with these children in mind that I wrote and illustrated my first books. I wanted them to feel proud of their own culture. It was important that their parents like the books, but it was even more important that their great-grandparents would smile, recognizing in my pictures and stories the proud old days which they knew about."

THE LESSONS OF MYTH

In 1977, Paul came to live permanently in the United States, first in South Dakota and later in Nebraska. A year later, he won the prestigious Caldecott Medal for *The Girl Who Loved Wild Horses*. It was all the encouragement he needed.

Paul has a great love for the mythology of the Plains Indians. In it, he finds many valuable lessons. "I think that most people today understand the word *myth* to mean fantasy, but that is exactly the opposite of what it was intended to mean," Paul contends. "All of the world's truths are conveyed in myths. More than just stories, the traditional Indian myths show us how older generations of Indians understood the world."

"For example, I know that the stars in the Big Dipper are millions of light-years away," Paul says. "Yet it's wonderful to think about the Indian belief that those stars are children who once lived here on earth. This myth inspired my book *Her Seven Brothers*."

Sometimes the myths are *parables*, or stories with moral lessons. Paul's book *Dream Wolf* is a kind of parable. Paul gives his interpretation of the story: "This is the lesson: The Creator made all things, and so room must be made for all things. We are part of a whole, and wolves too are a part of that whole."

Paul is saddened that modern man has brutally hunted and killed the wolf, driving the animal from its native territory. He contrasts this ruthlessness to the attitude of the Plains Indians, who felt grateful toward all the animals since they provided food. They believed all beings on the earth were connected as one. Paul concludes, "Where the wolf no longer roams he is missed by everything in nature. We feel his loss; creation is incomplete."

> **"As a child, I took the great Indian leaders of history as my heroes. Football players or pop-stars were too ordinary to be my heroes."**

In the preface to *Crow Chief*, Paul describes the buffalo days of the Plains Indians, before horses came to North America. He writes: "Indian people hunted buffalo because that was their main food. Hunting was work. People killed only what they needed. They had no concept of today's hunting for sport. They were in harmony with everything in nature, and had lived so for many thousands of years."

In his work, Paul Goble is, by his own admission, a fierce traditionalist. He strives to make every aspect of his books absolutely accurate. Paul says, "I make great efforts to get things right, both in words and pictures. I find it annoying to see illustrators who illustrate Native American scenes without any real knowledge behind what they are drawing."

To avoid mistakes, Paul, who has been adopted by the Yakima and Sioux tribes, relies on thorough research. He says, "I am writing and picturing things of more than 100 years ago. I have to know the museums well, and I revisit them again and again." Yet Paul's research amounts to more than hours spent hunched over ancient tomes in dusty libraries. Much of it is on-site; he often visits Indian reservations and encampments.

When Paul writes a story, his goal is to recreate the time when the tale was first told. He wants readers to feel as though they are in a tipi, years ago, with the storyteller seated before a glowing fire.

In keeping with Indian tradition, Paul adopts a direct writing style. He doesn't use a lot of adjectives or fancy flourishes to create atmosphere. Paul explains, "Indian storytellers were not descriptive. Instead, they would use a lot of movement to conjure up images. Gestures, many of which were connected to a universal sign language, would provide much of what critics call description. The spoken narrative itself was quite straightforward."

Paul sees his work as a way of giving back to the Indians treasures that were already theirs. By bringing a forgotten tale into the light, Paul helps to preserve a great and noble culture. His books offer a glimpse of what Native American life was like back in the buffalo days, when the Plains Indians were at their height. Paul concludes, "I have simply wanted to express and to share these things that I love so much."

THE GIRL WHO LOVED WILD HORSES
by PAUL GOBLE

Eloise Greenfield

BORN: May 17, 1929, in Parmele, North Carolina
HOME: Washington, D.C.

SELECTED TITLES

Rosa Parks
1973

She Come Bringing Me That Little Baby Girl
1974

Me and Neesie
1975

Africa Dream
1977

Honey, I Love and Other Love Poems
1978

Childtimes: A Three-Generation Memoir
1979

Grandmama's Joy
1980

Daydreamers
1981

Grandpa's Face
1988

Under the Sunday Tree
1988

Night on Neighborhood Street
1991

Through her many children's books, in both poetry and prose, Eloise Greenfield has made a profound and lasting contribution to children's literature.

As a writer, Eloise has always been motivated by a deep love for language. Intricately tied to this love is another even greater motivation. Eloise explains, "There's a desperate need for more black literature for children, for a large body of literature in which black children can see themselves and their lives and history reflected. I want to do my share in building it."

Eloise's books touch on recurring themes of family love and human relationships. She has written biographies about the lives and historical contributions of black Americans such as Rosa Parks and Paul Robeson. Her poetry celebrates the syntax of black language and cadence of black life. Speaking of the commitment she has to her work, Eloise says, "It is necessary for black children to have a true knowledge of their past and present, in order that they may develop an informed sense of direction for their future."

GROWING UP IN WASHINGTON, D.C.

Except for three months in Parmele, North Carolina, Eloise Greenfield has spent her entire life in Washington, D.C. She recalls: "When I was three months old, Daddy left home to make a way for us. He went North, as thousands of black people had done, during slavery and since. They went North looking for safety, for justice, for freedom, for work—for a good life. Often one member of a family would go ahead of the others to make a way—to find a job and a place to live. And that's what my father did."

The second oldest of five children, Eloise looks back on her childhood in Washington, D.C. with fondness. "Washington was much less populous then—it was almost rural," Eloise says. "There were vendors with horses and carts who came around selling vegetables and ice; there was the 'snowball man' who put fruit-flavored syrup on ice.

"We didn't have much money, but my father always had a job, and we were able to manage. He had an old car that he had to start with a crank, and we would all get in and go for a ride. We went to movies and to the Howard Theater, where great jazz musicians like Duke Ellington performed. Both of my parents loved the arts, so we were always doing something."

On her ninth birthday, Eloise and

her family moved into a new housing project named Langston Terrace. For Eloise, it was love at first sight. She remembers, "It was built on a hill, a group of tan brick houses and apartments with a playground as its center. The red mud surrounding the concrete walks had not yet been covered with black soil and grass seed, and the holes that would soon be homes for young trees were filled with rainwater. But it still looked beautiful to me.

"I want to choose and order words that children will want to celebrate. I want to make them shout and laugh and blink back tears and care about themselves."

"There were so many games to play and things to do. We played hide-and-seek at the lamppost, paddle tennis and shuffleboard, dodge ball and jacks. We danced in fireplug showers; jumped rope to rhymes; played Bouncy Bouncy Bally, swinging one leg over a bouncing ball; played baseball on a nearby field; had parties in the social room and bus trips to the beach."

Although childhood was a magical time, it was also touched by racism. "We knew about problems," Eloise says. "We heard about them, saw them, lived through some hard ones ourselves, but our community wrapped itself around us, put itself between us and the hard knocks, to cushion the blows.

"There were a lot of things we couldn't do and places we couldn't go. Washington was a city for white people. But inside that city, there was another city. It didn't have a name and it wasn't all in one area, but it was where black people lived."

For all of her life, as a citizen and as a writer, Eloise has identified with the black community. Her job always has been to try to make things better for friends, neighbors, family, and children. Eloise Greenfield has achieved this, most notably, through her books.

Eloise admits that writing was "the farthest thing from my mind when I was growing up. I loved words, but I loved to *read* them, not *write* them." While working at the U.S. Patent Office, though, Eloise got started writing. In 1963, she published her first poem. But she did not begin to write for children until after meeting Sharon Bell Mathis, a fellow member of the D.C. Black Writers Workshop.

Eloise says, "Sharon talked so passionately about the need for good black books that it was contagious. Once I realized the full extent of the problem, it became urgent for me to try, along with others, to build a large collection of books for children."

Eloise struggled with her craft, working late into the night. She methodically practiced the skills she'd need to become a professional writer. The hard work paid off. Since the early 1970s, Eloise Greenfield has been a major voice in children's literature. Her books celebrate the strength within each of us to overcome obstacles, the need for family togetherness in difficult times, and the transcendent power of language itself.

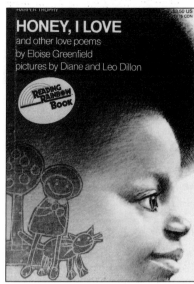

HARPER TROPHY $3.50 US
$4.75 CDN
HONEY, I LOVE
and other love poems
by Eloise Greenfield
pictures by Diane and Leo Dillon
READING RAINBOW BOOK

DO IT YOURSELF!

Eloise has written biographies of people whom she admires. She says, "I enjoyed doing them. The research is always interesting. I selected them because I felt they were people children needed to meet."

Whom do you admire? Write a brief biography of someone (it could be a famous person or a kind neighbor who lives down the street). Think of it as a way of introducing two friends: "Here's someone you should meet!"

Ruth Heller

BORN: April 2, 1924, in Winnipeg, Manitoba, Canada
HOME: San Francisco, California

SELECTED TITLES

"I have a tendency to overwork," Ruth Heller confesses.

"Every day is a work day. I get to my studio about 6:30 in the morning and I go home at about 9:00 at night. It's a long, long day but I love it. I find there are not enough hours in the day. On weekends my husband brings me breakfast in bed, then I go to work. I'll work until about 6:00. If I have a deadline, the work has to be done—and I *always* have a deadline.

"I've been interested in art for as long as I can remember," Ruth says with typical zeal. "I've always loved coloring and cutting and pasting and drawing—and generally making a big mess." Growing up, Ruth remembers copying comic strips from the newspaper. In school, she would always add a picture or two to her reports. She says, "I loved school. But it wasn't until the upper grades that I was able to study art."

After completing school, Ruth went on to become a designer and illustrator. She did all sorts of interesting work. Ruth recalls, "I began my career designing wrapping paper, cocktail napkins, kites, mugs, greeting cards, posters, and then coloring books." One day, a visit to an aquarium triggered an idea. Ruth decided to try her hand at writing.

Ruth recalls the day: "While researching at Steinhart Aquarium for a coloring book on tropical fish, I became intrigued with a strange looking shape floating in one of the tanks, and found that it was the egg sac of a dogfish shark. This led me to read about other egg-laying animals. My reading stimulated visions of colors and shapes and compositions. In addition to this visual wealth, I had found enough information to convince me that I wanted to write and illustrate a book."

Creating the book was easy compared to trying to sell it to a publisher. "It took me five years to get it published," Ruth says. "I contacted the most prestigious publishers in the world—and I have rejections from all of them!"

Part of the problem was that Ruth's style was so different from what people were used to. At that time, in the mid-70s, most nonfiction books for children were painfully boring. Then along came Ruth Heller with an entirely different approach. She not only used bright, beautiful illustrations, she wrote in rhyme! Ruth remembers, "Editors didn't know what to do with the book. I was told that children who'd enjoy the pictures were too young for the information. And that students who would be able to understand the vocabulary would find a picture book too babyish."

Luckily, one editor took a chance and published *Chickens Aren't the Only Ones.* Today, thanks to Ruth Heller and other innovative writers such as Gail Gibbons and Joanna Cole, children can read nonfiction books that are every bit as lively and imaginative as favorite storybooks.

RESEARCH, RHYMES, AND REVISION

Because Ruth does not have a strong background in science, she devotes long hours to research and relies on experts to make sure her facts are accurate. Ruth explains, "I'm constantly going back over my research and as I'm reading it triggers a vision of an illustration that I would like to do. It's a long process of making outlines and working up sketches. And it changes all the time!"

"I take my manuscripts to New York when they're finished. And I'm still changing words on my way to the publisher!"

What gives the books their visual freshness? "I try to make every page a complete surprise," Ruth says. "I make a tremendous effort not to repeat myself." To get started, Ruth needs to look at pictures of her subject. Ruth says, "I do everything. I go to the zoo and take pictures. I buy loads and loads of books and magazines. I keep a file of photographs I think I might need someday. I'm not good at imagining. I have to have either the actual object or a photograph in front of me. When I'm working from an actual object, I try to stick to it as closely as possible. But I never work from only one photograph. If it's an

ostrich, I try to get as many photographs as I can and surround myself with pictures of ostriches."

Sometimes Ruth works so hard she can't stop thinking about the book she's writing. She reveals, "I'm constantly thinking of the words and the rhymes. I'll fall asleep at night with the words swirling in my head and wake up in the morning and hopefully the words are still there."

As a child, Ruth liked reading books that rhymed, and later, as a parent, she enjoyed reading Dr. Seuss to her children. When it came time to write her own books, it seemed only natural to do it in rhyme. Ruth also thinks that rhymes make it easier for children to remember facts and acquire a bigger vocabulary. Equally important, the rhymes lend a playful quality to subjects that could otherwise be dull. Ruth says, "I've done five books on parts of speech. A lot of people think that's a pretty dry subject. Doing it in rhyme, with colorful illustrations, helps bring it to life."

Ruth offers this advice to young writers: "I think it's terribly important to read as much as you can. I don't think you can get much *out* of your head unless you put things *into* it. I also think it's very important to keep a journal."

What should you put into your journal? "Anything," Ruth answers. "Just like a diary, start with what you did that day. From there on, you'll find that the writing itself will open up all sorts of thoughts and feelings."

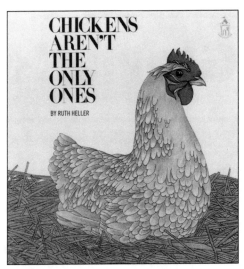

CHICKENS AREN'T THE ONLY ONES
BY RUTH HELLER

DO IT YOURSELF!

Ruth Heller finds writing in rhyme to be both challenging and fun. The challenge for Ruth is that her rhymes have to convey facts. Try it yourself. First, write down some simple directions, such as how to get to your house from school. Then try to get across the same information—but in *rhyme*. As Ruth might tell you, it may not be easy, but it sure will be fun!

Gloria Houston

BORN: November 24, year unavailable, in Marion, North Carolina
HOME: Tampa, Florida

SELECTED TITLES

The Year of the Perfect Christmas Tree: An Appalachian Story
1988

Littlejim
1990

My Great-Aunt Arizona
1992

But No Candy
1992

◇

For as long as Gloria Houston can remember, stories have played an important part in her life. "I was saturated with the language of everyday conversations and stories almost from birth," says the author.

Gloria grew up in a small town nestled in the forbidding beauty of the Appalachian mountains. It was a simple, rural way of life—full of colorful characters and strong traditions. Gloria's family still runs the country store where she grew up listening to people come and go, swapping stories of everyday events. But it was at home that Gloria was most "steeped in storytelling." Her father and mother loved to tell stories about the family and local history, and these tales have most influenced Gloria's work.

"Many of my books so far have been based on characters and incidents from Avery County, North Carolina, my childhood home," says Gloria. "*My Great-Aunt Arizona* is about my fourth-grade teacher and it's all true. *The Year of the Perfect Christmas Tree*, on the other hand, is all fiction, though I based it on people I know. I wrote it as a Christmas gift to my mother."

SHARING FAMILY STORIES

Gloria is proud of her Appalachian homeland. She says, "One of my goals as a writer is to help my young readers become acquainted with its wonderful culture.

"I always knew I would be a writer," Gloria reveals. "When I was seven, my Aunt Wilma gave me a copy of *Little Women*. In that book I found a kindred soul, Jo, and I knew that I would grow up to be like she was."

Nevertheless, it is one thing to be a writer and quite another to be a *published* writer. It took Gloria years of rejection before one of her books was accepted for publication. Gloria remembers, "*My Brother Joey Died* had 54 rejections. I still have them all in a file. It became like a game, 'Well, let's see how many more I can collect!'"

It was a heartbreaking time for the aspiring author. "Rejection was very difficult," Gloria admits. "Trying to get published was in part an attempt to build my self-esteem. What a way to build it—with 54 rejections! One way I dealt with it was to keep telling people that I was a writer. I told everybody who would listen: 'I'm a writer, I'm a writer, I'm going to be a writer.' And I wrote my little head off while I was saying it. I was trying to convince everybody else while

I was convincing me."

Gloria is fortunate to have a father and mother who continue to tell her stories. "My father, who is in his eighties now, is the local historian and storyteller. My mother has a sensory memory that is uncanny. She can recall colors, odors, small details unavailable in any published resource. When I am writing in the mountains, I run from my place down the hill to theirs constantly to ask them questions."

"I think that the stories within our families are an important part of who we are and give us a sense of belonging that few other things do."

Gloria believes that all families have meaningful stories to share. And like most folks in the Houston family, she tells a story to make her point: "Right at this moment," Gloria says, "I'm sitting on land that my great-great-great-great-great-grandfather, William Wiseman, got in a land grant from King George III of England. This land has been in my family for seven generations. If it weren't for the hill that's just to my right, I could see William Wiseman's grave. He was a stowaway on a ship from London at 13. My family has lived in this valley for that long. The oral stories that have been handed down in my family are no different from the oral stories in other families. It's just that we have the tradition of keeping them alive by telling them."

Gloria adds, "Outside of the Appalachian mountains, and outside some other parts of the South, most families don't sit around and tell those stories anymore. But they are there.

Those stories give you a sense of roots, a sense of belonging."

Readers of Gloria Houston's remarkable books will also come to know another important influence on her life—her Great-Aunt Arizona. Gloria, who like her great-aunt is a teacher, says, "Arizona was a remarkable woman and probably the greatest influence on my life. She truly lives on in what she gave to her students, including me. She spent her entire life teaching within five miles of her birthplace. And yet she has influenced the world through her students."

If there is a message in Gloria's writing, it may be that we should all value our own families, our own cultures, our own stories. Gloria loves to hear from young students who have asked their own parents to tell family stories. Gloria says with satisfaction, "Kids begin to look at their heritages. They begin to think, 'Hey, my family is special.' They begin to talk to their parents and their parents begin to talk to them. They come back with stories that no one ever thought to tell them."

And in all that talk, in all those stories, there just may be a book or two waiting for someone to write it down. Gloria Houston, through her books and her work, says that that someone could be you.

But No Candy

GLORIA HOUSTON · illustrated by LLOYD BLOOM

DO IT YOURSELF!

It might be fun to listen to, and write down, some of your own family stories. But Gloria admits that people aren't always ready to tell a story. They might not even know they have a story to tell. So Gloria offers this tip: "Here are a few specific questions to ask parents: What can you tell me about my grandmother? Where is my grandmother from? What did my grandmother do? These kinds of little questions will prompt stories—and stories are in every family."

AUTHOR

Tony Johnston

BORN: January 30, 1942, in Los Angeles, California
HOME: San Marino, California

SELECTED TITLES

The Vanished Pumpkin
1983

The Quilt Story
1985

Whale Song
1987

Pages of Music
1988

Yonder
1988

The Badger and the Magic Fan: A Japanese Folktale
1990

I'm Gonna Tell Mama I Want an Iguana
1990

Grandpa's Song
1991

Lorenzo the Naughty Parrot
1992

The Cowboy and the Blackeyed Pea
1992

◇

Tony Johnston is excited about a story. You can hear it in her voice. This is the part of the job she really loves—the thrill of a new idea and the challenge of making it all fall into place.

As she describes her story, Tony tells us a lot about the way she works. "I was in Tulsa recently," Tony says, "and heard an interesting fact about the Muscogee [Creek] tribe. When they were forced from their land in Alabama on a march to Tulsa in the 1830s, they brought living embers with them. The tribe relit the embers each night to remind them of their homeland."

Tony, who is part Cherokee and has a deep interest in Native American life, knew there was a story there somewhere. "I thought, 'Wow! This is a symbol for everybody who has ever had to leave his or her home behind.'"

Bursting with thoughts, Tony quickly jotted down a rough first draft. "That's the way I work," Tony says. "I try to grab the feeling when the idea strikes. I think I wrote most of the ember story on the airplane barf bag going home." Tony believes that in writing any story, the writer's own feelings must be involved. She explains, "If you get in touch with your emotions, you can write a first draft really without doing any research, then go back and fill it in. For me, going to the library and facing a mountain of research would get in the way of the creative process."

With a first draft in her hands, Tony can move on to the next stage. In this case, it meant doing some homework. Tony had a lot of questions she needed answered. She offers an example: "I wanted to know what a person from that tribe would have thought while standing at a grave site. If he were burying a relative, what would he be thinking? Who would he pray to? I know what a white person might think, but I don't know about a Creek." For help, Tony contacted the Muscogee tribe. The elders agreed to answer her questions.

But that's only one story of many that are in the works. When asked what else she's been up to lately, Tony answers with a laugh, "Oh, about 85 different things. I've always got a lot going." Tony, who has published more than 40 books, likes to work on many projects at the same time. But not all of them become published books. Tony admits, "I've got a lot of books going. But sometimes there comes a moment when I say, 'Enough. Nothing is going to happen here.' I mean, I've got a whole lot of good beginnings without middles or endings."

For those times when a story won't

flow, Tony has her own particular solution. "I've got a big silversmith's table with a huge drawer," Tony says. "I call it my 'drawer of dreams.' I stick in all my manuscripts that have come to a standstill. Someday, I hope I'll get back to those ideas."

FROM TEACHER TO WRITER

A former teacher, Tony used to create stories with her fourth-grade class. One day a friend encouraged Tony to try to get her stories published. "At the time, it hadn't occurred to me to become a children's book writer," Tony says. "I thought, 'Well, How do you do it?' I tried to figure out what makes one book wonderful and another only fair. And, of course, I'm *still* trying to figure that out."

> ### "I think of myself as a soup pot. You throw all of this stuff into the pot and let it blub around, and just maybe you'll end up with a good soup!"

A lot of Tony's writing time is actually spent rewriting. "I revise and revise and revise," Tony says. "I'm so picky. *Yonder* took me seven years to write. That book meant a lot to me. I wanted it to be perfect." Tony does not illustrate her books, so she depends upon her editor to select an artist who will do a good job at bringing her words to life. Tony has been fortunate to work with such great illustrators as Tomie dePaola, Lillian Hoban, Ed Young, Margot Tomes, Leo Politi, Victoria Chess, and Lloyd Bloom. To each one, she is grateful.

It becomes clear in speaking with Tony that *Yonder* holds special meaning for her. She tries to explain why: "I cried for about seven years while I was writing that book. Everything that you write is autobiographical. I don't care if it's about snakes or iguanas, it is always rooted in something that means something to you. *Yonder* evokes so many things from my childhood. I spent a lot of time on a ranch growing up. I was very close to my grandparents. Somehow I tried to put all of that family feeling into the book. One of my grandparents, Addie, was from Texas. Whenever I would ask, 'Grandma, where's my sister?' she would answer, 'Yonder.' When I started writing, that word triggered more and more memories."

The creative process, for Tony, is a mystery that is beyond understanding. How you make the leap from *The Princess and the Pea* to the *Cowboy and the Blackeyed Pea* represents the magical element of writing. But she tells a story that provides a clue: "Recently my husband and I were driving in Idaho and Wyoming. We were driving down the road, and everything was covered with snow and sagebrush. I was looking into the empty fields. And the more I looked, the more things I could see. At one point, I said, 'Roger, look at all those pronghorn!' He looked, but saw only sagebrush and snow. I guess that's the way I think about these stories. They are all out there, but you really have to look closely. There are always stories. You could walk around the block and find a story. It's the way you are in tune with the world around you that makes the difference."

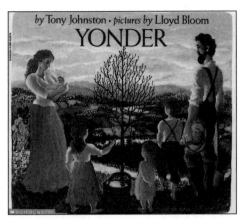

by Tony Johnston · pictures by Lloyd Bloom
YONDER

DO IT YOURSELF!

Tony Johnston talks about her drawer of dreams, the secret place where she keeps all of her thoughts, dreams, and manuscripts. Find your own special place—it can be a box, a drawer, a folder, a journal—where you can keep your ideas and cherished objects. Who knows—you may open it one day and find a story waiting for you!

Karla Kuskin

BORN: July 17, 1932, in New York, New York
HOME: Brooklyn, New York

Can you imagine what it feels like to be the last leaf on a tree in autumn, silently letting go and drifting to the ground? Can you imagine what it feels like to be a snake, a strawberry, or a sled? Karla Kuskin can.

A poet and author of more than 40 books for children, Karla often plays pretend to help her write poems. In an introduction to one of her books, *Any Me I Want to Be*, Karla explains the process this way: "Instead of describing how a cat, the moon, or a pair of shoes appears to me, I have tried to get inside each subject and briefly be it.

"I do that," Karla says, "because I did it as a child. I remember when I was about four, I was absolutely stunned with this idea that I was *in* myself. How had I gotten into this person? How did it happen? As a very little child, I found that baffling, and very interesting. I think that must have lead to the question: *What would it feel like to be something else*?"

Karla also feels that this imaginary activity is a great way to learn. She says, "If you are able to imagine being someone else, it helps you understand people who are different. It helps you see the world through someone else's eyes." Our imagination, Karla emphasizes, allows us to realize that different lives are just as valuable as our own.

Through sense and silliness, bouncy rhymes and flowing rhythms, Karla shares her love of poetry with young children. A mood, a memory, a sound—anything can spark a poem. And anyone can write one, Karla believes. "Poetry can be as natural and effective a form of self-expression as singing or shouting," she says.

Karla has always loved the music of language, the rhythm of words. She thinks this is from her childhood. She states, "I am a firm believer in reading aloud because, I suppose, I loved it so much as a child." Grateful for a childhood in which reading was an everyday family activity, Karla believes that "when you are exposed to poetry when you are little, it stays with you for the rest of your life.

"When I am working on a book of poetry," Karla says, "I jot down everything on any scrap of paper at hand. I pay attention to what's going through my head. I'm much more aware of language, words, rhythm, description. I try to hang on to these ideas, because if I don't write them down, they're gone forever."

But where does a poet *get* ideas? Where does Karla find her poems? "Everywhere," Karla says, "anywhere." The important thing is to pay attention to what's around you. Karla offers this advice: "Get used to looking around you, paying attention to small details.

> ## "The words in a poem are like the colors in a painting. When they are put together with care, they make an engaging picture."

"It's a tough world out there. It can be very difficult, very unpoetic. Yet if you look, there are things to see that have poetry in them. If you *really* keep your eyes open and you *really* listen to language, you discover that there's a tremendous amount of beauty, too."

It is Karla's hope that readers of her poems will, in turn, write poems of their own. As Karla says, "If you read, you write." Karla realizes, though, that most children will not grow up to become professional writers. The important thing about writing, Karla says, is that it helps the writer discover his or her own thoughts and feelings.

"In difficult times," Karla confides, "I've always found that to write out what I feel is very helpful. I put it down and I begin to understand it better."

WORKING WITH WORDS
In its basic form, revision is a simple process of messing around with words. The writer takes words away, eliminates unnecessary paragraphs, smooths out rhythms, searches for the very best word.

Yet revision is often more than just tinkering around with words. It is sometimes a matter of looking at an old story or poem with new eyes. It can be a time to make sweeping changes—rethink the plot, change the setting, introduce new characters. That's the process which helped Karla Kuskin finally publish one of her most famous books, *The Philharmonic Gets Dressed*.

Karla remembers: "When I first wrote *The Philharmonic Gets Dressed*, I wrote it with only one musician and it wasn't interesting. I put the manuscript away for a couple of years. Then all of a sudden I realized the book might work if it was about the whole orchestra."

Once married to an oboe player, Karla got the idea by noticing her children watch their father get dressed for work. Karla wanted to present these gifted musicians as regular people with real jobs—just like carpenters, bus drivers, and football players.

"What I was saying was: Here are people who get up, get washed, get dressed—just like you do—but what they do for work is heavenly. But it isn't play. It is real, true, serious work."

Maybe the same can be said for children's authors like Karla Kuskin. They awake in the morning, eat breakfast, wash the dishes, and go off to work. Their work is to imagine and feel, to write and draw, to create beautiful books. Not a bad job if you can get it. But as Karla might point out—it's still work.

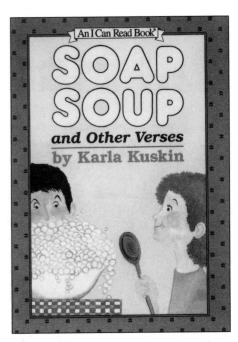

> ## DO IT YOURSELF!
> Karla wrote notes that accompany her poems in *Near the Window Tree*. These notes show where Karla got some of the ideas for her poems. Try taking some notes yourself—maybe it will help start a poem or two! Karla sometimes looks to a tree for inspiration: "Once in a while I look out at the tree in the yard. Then I look at the blank paper on my lap and I try to get the tree to give me an idea for something to write about."

Bill Martin, Jr.

BORN: March 20, 1916, in Hiawatha, Kansas
HOME: New York, New York

SELECTED TITLES

Brown Bear, Brown Bear, What Do You See?
1971

The Ghost-Eye Tree
1985

Barn Dance!
1986

White Dynamite and Curly Kidd
1986

Here Are My Hands
1987

Knots on a Counting Rope
1987

Chicka Chicka Boom Boom
1989

The Magic Pumpkin
1989

Polar Bear, Polar Bear, What Do You Hear?
1991

◇

Born in 1916, Bill Martin, Jr. remembers growing up in the days before television, during a time when kids had to create their own entertainment. Bill vividly recalls, "On long summer nights the kids in the neighborhood would sit on the curb underneath the street lights, telling stories to one another. Most of them were ghost stories. We loved those."

Bill wrote his first book as a favor for his brother, Bernard, who was an artist. "I was in the army," Bill recalls. "It was 1944. My brother had been injured in the service. He wrote to me and said, 'Why don't you write me a children's story so I can illustrate it while I'm recuperating.' I said, 'Sure.'" One Sunday, Bill sat down at the typewriter and banged out a story called *The Little Squeegy Bug*. Bernard liked it, illustrated it, and had it published!

Encouraged by this success, Bill and Bernard started their own publishing company. But Bill soon realized that he didn't know enough about children. So he went off to school to study early childhood education. After graduation, Bill became a principal at an elementary school. In 1960 Bill joined the publishing house of Holt, Rinehart & Winston as an editor and creator of school reading materials.

"I started writing the kinds of things that I thought children needed," Bill says. More than anything, he wanted children to love books. He says, "I wanted children to become page-turners. I wanted them to be able to read a book in five minutes, so they could proudly say, 'I read a book.' Children love to have power over books. When a frail reader finds a book that he or she can read, it's such a triumph that the reader will read it again and again and again."

BROWN BEAR AND MORE

More often than not, writing is a matter of hard work and endless revision. But sometimes, amazingly, the words flow easily and they are exactly right from the very beginning. Bill recalls one such instance: "I was on the train one day, coming into work from suburban New York. I heard, '*Brown bear, brown bear, what do you see?*' So I wrote it down. Having no tablet with me, I wrote it on the newspaper. Then I wrote, '*I see a red bird looking at me.*' Then I wrote down 'yellow duck,' 'blue horse,' 'green frog,' 'purple cat,' 'white dog,' etc. Within 15 minutes, the story was complete."

Excited, Bill immediately typed up the story when he reached the office.

Now he needed to find an illustrator. Thumbing through a magazine, Bill was struck by an ad for a pharmaceutical company. "It had a collage of a beautiful pink lobster," Bill recalls. "I said to myself, 'That's the guy who should illustrate the book.'"

"No reading lesson is complete unless it leaves children with the sharp taste of words lingering on their tongues."

◇

The name of the illustrator was Eric Carle. At the time, he had never done a children's book. Bill asked Eric: "Are you interested in illustrating a children's book?" Eric cautiously answered: "Probably so." And that is the story of how the great Eric Carle, author of *The Very Hungry Caterpillar*, got started in children's books.

These days, Bill works with a co-author named John Archambault. Bill explains how the partnership works: "We get an idea for a story. Sometimes it's only a line or two. For example, with *Knots on a Counting Rope*, John and I decided that we wanted to express a close relationship between a grandfather and a boy. Later, to add conflict to the story, we decided that the boy should be blind. Then both of us started putting together notions."

Bill believes that having a creative partner can help make for a better book. He offers this example: "When we did *Knots on a Counting Rope*, I thought it was ready to go to the publisher. Then John called me and said, 'Bill, I don't think that story is finished. We say the boy is blind, but we don't show it.' So we started considering what we should do to show the blindness. John finally suggested, 'What if we have the boy say: "Horses I know, Grandfather, but

what is blue?"'" Then we wrote that episode of about 14 lines. I thought the story was ready to go. But John called again. He said, 'We say the boy overcame his blindness, but we don't show it.' That's when we decided to put in the race." Bill concludes: "That's the advantage of a partner—it's like having an editor as well!"

One of Bill's most popular books, *Chicka Chicka Boom Boom*, features a jazzy rhyme that invites children to guess the next word or phrase. The snappy rhymes and memorable patterns allow children to read along and share the experience.

Many writers talk about how it sometimes takes years for an idea to become a fully developed book. That was the case with *Chicka Chicka Boom Boom*. Bill explains, "*Chicka Chicka Boom Boom* was carried around as a single line in our journals for a couple of years. We didn't do anything with it; it just sort of slept there."

Weeks, months, and years passed. One day Bill got a call from a publisher who needed a story for a textbook—and *fast*. Though Bill didn't have any stories ready to offer, he pretended that he did. Bill recalls, "I said, 'Yup, I can have it to you in two weeks.' So I opened my journal and rediscovered that line: '*A told B and B told C, I'll race you to the top of the coconut tree*.' John and I wrote the first half of it, when all the letters went up the tree—'chicka chicka boom boom'—and it ended there. Then a different publisher wanted it as a children's book, but said they needed 32 pages. That's when we wrote the second half."

by Bill Martin, Jr. and John Archambault illustrated by Lois Ehlert

DO IT YOURSELF!

Like Bill Martin, Jr. and John Archambault, try writing with a partner. You'll need to talk a lot in the beginning, sharing ideas until you agree on what the story should be about. One approach might be to write it as a dialogue, like *Knots on a Counting Rope*. Each writer can take on the voice of a character. But as you write, continue to share ideas and make suggestions to improve the story. Remember, it's important to *respect* each other along the way.

Jean Marzollo

BORN: June 24, 1942, in Manchester, Connecticut
HOME: Cold Spring, New York

As a child, when Jean Marzollo wasn't playing ball or riding her bike, she was probably off with friends making doll clothes. "We were always making things," Jean fondly recalls. "During the summer we would sit under the trees and sew for hours."

Jean likens her experience making clothes to her current life as a writer. She says, "I never thought about being an author when I was young, but the pleasure I now take in making books is the same pleasure I took as a child making doll clothes. The creative process is essentially the same. First, you think of something you want to make, next you plan how you'll do it, and then you do it."

After graduating from college, Jean first worked as a teacher and then as a freelance writer and editor. In 1972, Jean accepted a job that would change her life. She became the editor of *Let's Find Out*, a magazine for children in kindergarten. Over the next 20 years, Jean helped make *Let's Find Out* a fun-filled, award-winning magazine. In doing so, Jean came to understand a lot about how children learn. This knowledge has helped her immeasurably as the author of more than 60 books.

Working on *Let's Find Out*, Jean had to stay up-to-date on children's books. She noticed that there weren't any good books on Christopher Columbus for young children. "I worried about how to do it for a long time," Jean remembers. "Then I realized the perfect solution was to keep going with the rhyme that everybody knows: '*In fourteen hundred ninety-two/Columbus sailed the ocean blue.*'" Beginning with that famous line, she spun off a simple rhyming tale based on Columbus's great adventure and called it "*In 1492.*"

Like many writers, Jean believes it's important to jot down ideas right away. She ruefully admits, "I've learned the hard way that if I don't write my ideas down, I forget them." She saves these ideas—they could be as simple as a rhyme scribbled on a scrap of paper—and files them into folders. Jean depends on these folders for inspiration. "I can't sit down and say, 'Today I'm going to write a picture book.' When I'm stuck for an idea, I look through the files I keep. I can't make ideas happen. Ideas usually come to me while I'm doing other things."

HARD WORK AND GOOD LUCK

Over the past few years, Jean has enjoyed great success with her best-selling *I Spy* books. "It's just luck, really," Jean modestly claims. "You can't really tell which books will sell. You just have to follow your heart and do what's next."

The *I Spy* books grew directly from Jean's days with *Let's Find Out* magazine. Carol Devine Carson and Jean had asked a wonderful photographer, Walter Wick, to shoot some posters for the magazine. The posters turned out beautifully. They were so original, in fact, that two editors at Scholastic urged Walter, Carol, and Jean to collaborate on a book.

Jean explains how the books are made: "First we discuss various possibilities for scenes. Walter then begins his elaborate imaginative process. For most of the pictures, he devises a set using whatever is needed: blocks, toys, scraps of wood, old shelves, a window frame, chicken wire, fabric, pillow stuffing. Next, he carefully places objects into the scene, many of which he hides."

Jean and Walter speak with each other on the phone throughout the photographic process. Looking at Polaroid test photos, they make sure that there are many objects in each picture—cleverly hidden—that rhyme. Walter then takes the final photo and sends a copy to Jean. With photo in hand, Jean writes the final rhymes.

Jean likes to work on several books at the same time. One week it's a nonfiction biography; the following week she might be working on a book of rhymes. Then the next week (or day!) she might switch to a chapter book for slightly older readers. "That way, if I get stuck," Jean explains, "I can put one project aside and move to another."

One of Jean's proudest achievements is the *39 Kids on the Block* series. In these delightful stories, Jean made it a point to represent children from different ethnic backgrounds. Jean explains how some careful research helped make her books even better: "The second book was about Christmas. I asked myself, 'How do Native Americans celebrate Christmas?'" Jean got in touch with an early childhood expert in Nebraska who is also a Native American. Jean recalls, "She understood my need to have authentic details for my book. She told me the story of her son, John Beane, who was given an eagle feather as a baby because he was born very small and weak. The eagle feather symbolizes strength, and John Beane grew up to be strong. Now, every year at Christmas, his family puts that eagle feather on the top of their tree."

Real world research like Jean's makes an important difference. In the case of John Beane, the actual details anchor the book (*The Best Present Ever*) in reality— teaching us about Native American traditions without making stereotypical assumptions about people. "Besides," Jean frankly adds, "it was such a wonderful story, I just *had* to use it."

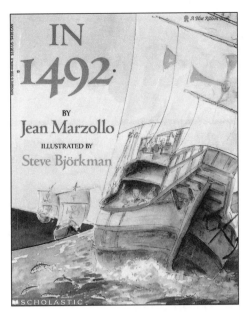

IN 1492
BY Jean Marzollo
ILLUSTRATED BY Steve Björkman

SCHOLASTIC

J. Brian Pinkney

BORN: August 28, 1961, in Boston, Massachusetts
HOME: Brooklyn, New York

SELECTED TITLES

The Boy and the Ghost
1989

The Ballad of Belle Dorcas
1990

Sukey and the Mermaid
1992

Happy Birthday, Martin Luther King
1993

Max Found Two Sticks
1993

What inspired J. Brian Pinkney to take his career as an artist in a new direction? A fondness for drum playing. "I've always played drums," Brian explains, "and I've always wanted to illustrate a book about a drummer. Finally I realized if I wanted to do it, I'd have to write the book myself."

At first, the thought of writing his own book made Brian uneasy. "It was kind of scary," Brian admits. "I never considered myself to be a writer—I was an artist. And artists were on one side and writers were on the other. But I did know that I was something of a storyteller. I thought, 'Well, I can always learn.'"

Fortunately for Brian, his wife, Andrea, is a talented editor and writer for *Essence* magazine and a children's book writer. Brian would write in bits and pieces, sharing the work with Andrea along the way. "You can do it," she told him, "you can write." Her encouragement helped Brian believe in himself as a writer, and before too long he finished *Max Found Two Sticks*.

LIKE FATHER, LIKE SON

If Brian's last name has a familiar ring, it may be because you've heard of his dad, Jerry Pinkney, the award-winning illustrator of such books as *The Patchwork Quilt*, *Mirandy and Brother Wind*, and *The Talking Eggs*. Brian cheerfully admits to following in his father's footsteps. "When I was growing up," Brian says, "my father did a lot of advertising and editorial work, as well as books. Because my father was an artist, I wanted to be like him. He was my idol."

Brian is glad to have a father who can give him advice about the art he creates. "There's no competition between us," Brian states. "It's a friendship. That's probably because he is *such* a nice guy. He never tried to tell me, 'This is how you make pictures.' He was always very supportive of whatever I did."

As an African-American artist in a field which has been dominated by white illustrators, Brian brings an added sense of responsibility to his work. "For me," Brian explains, "the whole push for multicultural literature is an effort to compensate for all the years of *not* focusing on the contributions of other ethnic groups to America." Yet Brian points out that he's only doing what's natural for him. "It's kind of like a writer who writes from his own experiences," Brian says. "I'm illustrating out of my own experiences and my own heritage—it's like I'm covering thousands of years in terms of a black culture that hasn't really been expressed. Besides," he adds, "my work is so personal, I feel like I'm doing books about me."

As a child, Brian attended mostly white schools. He jokes, "I went to integrated schools—but they weren't integrated until I got there!" At home, Brian's family made sure to learn about and celebrate their cultural background. But school was a different world: "In school, I was black and the rest of the world was white," Brian recalls. "We spent about one week on black history. I was so self-conscious during that one week because everything was directed to me, or at least I felt that way. So by doing books like *The Ballad of Belle Dorcas*, it's my chance to catch up on my own heritage."

Brian recently completed a book that had special meaning for him, *Happy Birthday, Martin Luther King* by Jean Marzollo. Brian says, "I went down to Atlanta and visited the actual house in which he was born. I wanted to keep the book simple, but at the same time I wanted it to be monumental in feeling." To achieve this feeling, Brian drew the illustrations so that readers are always looking up at the figures in the book.

"My generation is the generation that came right after the civil rights movement. A lot of the opportunities I've had were because of Martin Luther King's work. He opened up so many doors for me and for so many other children."

In most of his books, Brian uses an illustrative technique called scratchboard. Brian describes how he discovered this unique approach: "When I was doing my first picture book, *The Boy and the Ghost*, I decided that the way I was doing my artwork wasn't satisfying to me. I was feeling that I wanted something else out of my artwork, but I didn't know what it was."

by Jean Marzollo • Illustrated by J. Brian Pinkney

At the advice of a teacher, Brian began to fool around with the scratchboard process. "I fell in love with it," Brian says. Working on scratchboard offers a sense of rhythm that pleases Brian the drum enthusiast. "There's always sound when I'm scratching. I lay down the lines in patterns. It's like doing a drumroll. You can't think about how many times the sticks hit the drum. It's like: Ch-ch, ch-ch, ch-ch. When I'm scratching, I often play music in the background. I'm just putting down rhythm. I like the sound it makes; it's part of the whole process."

DO IT YOURSELF!

Study the illustrations in Brian's books (*The Ballad of Belle Dorcas* and *Sukey and the Mermaid* are fine examples). Now try your own scratchboard illustrations— all you need are paper, a black crayon, and an artist's knife. Just put a layer of black crayon on a piece of paper and scratch into it. If you'd like to try Brian's technique, get a piece of white illustration board and cover it with black ink. After the ink dries, scratch into it with the knife. "There are also two scratchboard nibs you can buy in an art supply store," Brian adds. "One looks like an arrowhead and the other looks like a spoon."

Patricia Polacco

Born: July 11, 1944, in Lansing, Michigan
Home: Oakland, California

SELECTED TITLES

Meteor!
1987

The Keeping Quilt
1988

Rechenka's Eggs
1988

Uncle Vova's Tree
1989

Babushka's Doll
1990

Just Plain Fancy
1990

Thunder Cake
1990

Applemando's Dreams
1991

Some Birthday!
1991

Chicken Sunday
1992

Mrs. Katz and Tush
1992

Picnic at Mudsock Meadow
1992

The Bee Tree
1993

Patricia Polacco grew up listening to the wonderful stories of her parents and grandparents, her head swimming with vivid images and characters. "My fondest memories," she recalls, "are of sitting around a stove or open fire, eating apples and popping corn while listening to the old ones [her grandparents] tell glorious stories about the past."

Patricia was born in Lansing, Michigan. Her parents divorced when she was three years old and her brother, Richard, was seven. Patricia recalls, "Even though my parents lived apart, they both were very involved in our lives. We spent the school year with my mother and her parents on a small farm in Union City, Michigan, and the summers with my father in Williamston, Michigan."

In all of her books—as in her life—Patricia Polacco makes it clear that family roots are important. "The old ones" provided most of the inspiration for her stories. Patricia says, "Babushka [Grandma] and her family came from the Ukraine, just outside of Kiev in Russia. My Diadushka [Grampa] came from Soviet Georgia. My mother's parents were great historians, but they also took us to the world of fancy and magic with stories. People on both sides of my family saw perfectly ordinary events as miraculous. And without this appreciation of even the smallest, tenderest little thing, you're doomed."

As a writer and illustrator, Patricia brings this same sense of appreciation to her books. She's equally comfortable weaving a colorful yarn based upon her Russian heritage as retelling an event from her childhood. Her stories are rich in cultural detail and filled with characters of different ages, races, and religions. And always, there is a deep pleasure in very simple things. "You have to look for the miracles in very ordinary events," Patricia insists.

At the age of seven, Patricia moved with her mother to Oakland, California, returning to Michigan every summer to spend time with her father. Oakland was an exciting place for young Patricia, filled with a diverse array of people. She still lives there. With obvious pride, Patricia describes her neighborhood: "We live in a urban mixed neighborhood, which means that my neighbors come in as many colors, ideas, and belief systems as there are people on this planet."

Patricia derives great satisfaction from seeing different cultures come together in mutual understanding.

"Instead of separating and pulling apart, we should be uniting and pulling together," she says. This theme is sounded again and again in her stories. Most recently, Patricia completed a story about the Oakland fire of 1991. The devastating brush fire killed 25 people and destroyed over 3,400 homes. Yet even amidst this despair, Patricia found reason for hope.

> ## "When I'm home I'm usually in sweats and gym shoes, my hair barely combed, and I'll be drenched with perspiration after sitting and thinking."

"Nothing brought us closer together than the terrible tragedy of the Oakland fire," she says. "We literally watched our homes burn down. Everyone, regardless of color, age or economic background, reached out to help those in need. Strangers were hugging in the streets. The support was remarkable. It's just a shame that it takes a tragedy to bring out the essential goodness in all of us."

ROCKING AROUND THE CLOCK

Early each morning, Patricia, dressed in a comfortable sweatsuit, will sit in a rocking chair and rock rhythmically, back and forth. This is her time—a time for gathering energy, thoughts, and dreams.

Patricia says of her daily habit: "I had a wonderful childhood, but the only pain I had was out of my inability to do schoolwork easily. I have dyslexia and dysnumeria. In my dreams, of course, I was perfect. Rocking was something that I did that made me feel whole. And it's carried over into my adult life. My husband and kids could tell you—there's a couple of hours in the morning and sometimes in the evening when I just need to rock.

"When I am composing a story, I sit in one of my rocking chairs and dream it up. For me, rocking is important to the process. I have 12 rocking chairs in the house, and I keep small pads and pens next to them, in case a real good idea springs into my head."

According to Patricia, the most important aspect of storytelling is to write with honest emotions. Her advice is clear and direct: "*Write about things that you really experience!* When the story has a great deal of meaning for you, it very probably will have meaning for others as well."

Patricia's success has given her the opportunity to visit with children in schools across the country. She says, "That's the whole reason for doing this work. If I couldn't be around children, there would almost be no point.

"I really like being around kids. I like to touch 'em, I like to smell 'em, I like to catch colds from 'em, I like to hear what they have to say. Plus, in their eyes you see the hope of the world. It gives you the courage to go on and live your life in a world that appears to have gone mad."

DO IT YOURSELF!

Patricia tells how she got the idea for *The Keeping Quilt*: "One day I took out our quilt and said, 'I want to draw every situation in our family that this quilt has been witness to.' So I drew them and that's how the book began." Try it yourself. Think of an item in your house— perhaps a mirror or a favorite chair—and draw pictures of different scenes in your family history that it has witnessed. You just might end up with a story or two!

Jack Prelutsky

BORN: September 8, 1940, in Brooklyn, New York
HOME: Mercer Island, Washington

Poet Jack Prelutsky confesses, "I'm a compulsive and constant notetaker. I always have a notebook with me because I'm always seeing things. The most asked question is always, 'How do you get your ideas?' I find it impossible *not* to have ideas! I have ideas because I'm alive. As long as I keep my senses alert and remain open to the world, the ideas continue to flow."

Jack, a former photographer (*and* cab driver, *and* busboy, *and* furniture mover, *and* potter, *and* folksinger), compares taking notes with taking photographs. He says that when he shoots a roll of 36 pictures, only about 10 percent will turn out to be good photographs. "It's the same thing with taking notes," Jack patiently explains. "I don't know ahead of time which of my notes are going to turn into a poem. A note can be anything. It can be a funny name, a joke, something I overheard, an idea that popped into my mind, a rhyme, an idea for a new game—there are no rules. My only rule is: *Write it down immediately.* Because if I don't, I'll forget it."

Unlike many writers who practically chain themselves to their desks each morning, Jack works when he's inspired. "I can go for days, even months, without writing at all," the poet admits. "There are times when I have no more need to write than the butcher or the guy next door. But one day I will wake up and sort of say, 'Today.' Then I do a complete turnaround. I become obsessed with writing. I write around the clock. I live in my pajamas. I become an impossible person. I work and work, 16 or 18 hours in a row. I'll do this for weeks at a time."

AT FIRST, POETRY WAS BORING

As a boy growing up in The Bronx, New York, Jack found that poetry—or at least the poetry he was taught in school—was a lot like liver. "I simply couldn't stand the stuff," Jack says with distaste. "I was told that it was good for me, but I wasn't convinced."

The problem was, the teachers in school only taught very old poetry that was written by, well, dead people. Jack stresses that he has nothing against dead people—"I don't blame them," Jack says, "it's not their fault they're dead." It was just that the poems had nothing to do with his everyday life.

Jack wondered why there couldn't be other types of poems. He says, "What about poems about the New York Yankees? Or my friend, the guy who would eat anything if you gave him enough money? I did write a poem about that, by the way, 'Baloney Belly Billy' in *The New Kid on the Block*":

He swallows anything for cash:
For a dollar he will gladly
eat a lizard off a fence,
just imagine what he'd swallow
for another fifty cents.

"If I wanted to hear a poem, it would have been nice to hear poems I related to, such as poems about people like myself, or things that I enjoyed—sports, dinosaurs, dragons—the things kids think about."

Today, Jack is one of the most popular poets writing for children. When Jack reads his poetry aloud to children, he tries to make it exciting. "A poem is a living thing," Jack states. "It comes from a living person. So when you present a poem, you should put the same amount of effort into it as the poet did when he was writing it. I sing poems, I jump up and down, I use props, anything that will help make it come alive. The thing is, it's not boring. Poetry is fun."

Sitting in his studio, a room crammed with more than 3,000 poetry books for children, Jack often starts the writing day with a few warm-up exercises. Like an athlete stretching before a game, Jack limbers up his mind before writing. He plays word games on his computer. He fills in a crossword puzzle. He makes up a list of silly, ridiculous names. It gets his creative juices flowing.

Because he is asked the question so often, Jack makes a great effort to explain, honestly and sincerely, where his ideas come from. "Everything I see or hear can become a poem," Jack offers. "When I was a kid, there was a worm-eating contest in my neighborhood. That became a poem called 'Willie Ate a Worm,' which appears in *Rolling Harvey Down the Hill*. I ate in a diner that had awful food. This became 'Gussie's Greasy Spoon' in *The New Kid on the Block*."

It's fascinating to hear Jack give a detailed description of his creative process. Here's how one poem got started: "I was in the market buying some boneless breasts of chicken and I suddenly asked myself, 'What about the rest of the chicken? Was that boneless too?' All right, so now I take out my notebook and write it down: 'Boneless chicken. Think about it.' So now I take the idea: Yes, there is such a thing as a boneless chicken. I don't have to make up any more silly things, because all I have to do is pretend I'm a reporter and ask that boneless chicken some basic questions, such as who, why, what, where, when, what if, and why not. For example, I wondered what sort of egg a boneless chicken would lay. First I thought, a boneless egg. But eggs *are* boneless, so that's not funny. Then one day I was having scrambled eggs for breakfast. There it was, the ending for my poem!"

"For me, revising is part of the whole process. It's learning."

DO IT YOURSELF!

Jack Prelutsky thinks that poetry can be fun. More than fun, it should be a rip-roaring good time. So why not throw a poetry party. Here's Jack's idea: "Have a 'Something Big' party. Children can dress up in oversized clothing such as novelty eyeglasses, huge neckties, hats, and shoes. Kids can bring in oversized cookies and other big foods for refreshments."

Faith Ringgold

BORN: October 8, 1930, in Harlem, New York
HOME: Harlem, New York

SELECTED TITLES

Tar Beach
(Caldecott Honor Book)
1991

Aunt Harriet's Underground Railroad in the Sky
1992

To hear Faith Ringgold tell it, she had a storybook childhood. Faith describes those days, growing up in Harlem, New York, during the 1930s, with infectious enthusiasm: "My childhood was magical," she says. "I had a great time."

Faith was the baby in a family with an older brother and sister. Her parents were hard-working people, determined to provide their children with a positive environment and a quality education.

Faith recalls, "My childhood was the most wonderful period of my life—till now. Though I was often home sick with asthma, I had a lot of time to be alone with my parents and be creative with art and fabrics. Mother took me to see the great performers of the time—Billie Holiday and Duke Ellington, among others—and to museums and public landmarks like the Statue of Liberty. She put me in touch with the best."

STORY QUILTS

Faith was fortunate. Even during the Great Depression, her father managed to hold a job and keep food on the table. Faith remembers childhood friends who didn't have it so easy. "I still remember the day I was tripping home from school with a friend. We walked by some household belongings piled in the street and my friend said, 'That's my doll! These are my things!' Her family had been evicted."

Thinking back to that time, remembering the warm sense of community she enjoyed, Faith is quick to add: "Neighbors took them in. That's what we did in those days; we took care of our friends. We didn't leave them homeless in the street."

From an early age, Faith benefited from two family traditions that would help her career as an artist in years to come. First, there was storytelling. "Everyone was a storyteller when I was a child," Faith says. "The stories told to me when I was a little girl weren't folktales. They were real tales about real people's lives. Our families wanted to tell us what life was really like, what it took to survive."

The next important tradition was sewing. Faith relates how the skill was passed on from generation to generation: "My mother was a dressmaker and fashion designer. She taught me to sew and to love fabrics. She learned to sew from her mother, who in turn learned from her mother, and so on back to my great-great-grandmother, Susie Shannon, who was a slave. She worked making quilts for the plantation owners."

Bursting with a desire to express herself through art, Faith was determined, from a very early age, to become an artist—one way or another. She graduated from the City College of New York in 1950. To make ends meet, she taught art in the New York City public schools from 1955 to 1973. All during that time, Faith kept painting away, producing new and exciting artwork. "I always saw myself," she reflects, "as an artist who taught art." She adds, "That's the point of being an artist. You can communicate things that you feel and see. You are a voice. Once art is made, it can be seen. That is a very powerful thing."

> ## "My fondest memories of growing up in Harlem are the people. People on my street, people in my building, friends of mine I saw every day."

Gradually, Faith began experimenting with a new art form called "story quilts"—works that combine painting, sewing, different fabrics, and storytelling. A story quilt looks like an ordinary patchwork quilt. It is made in the traditional way, with patches of cloth sewn together. But in Faith's quilts, she added panels with words, while other panels contained illustrations. In a way, they were like picture books on blankets!

Finally, Faith—just like everyone else in her family—was telling stories of her own. She thought back on her childhood in Harlem. She remembered family stories about racial injustice and inequality. And she wrote what was in her heart.

Faith says, "I never knew until 1989 that I would—or could—write

and illustrate children's books. Andrea Cascardi, who was an editor at Crown publishers at the time, called me to say she had seen a poster of my painted story quilt 'Tar Beach.' She had read the story on the quilt and thought it would make a good children's book." Faith signed a book contract and painted new illustrations to accompany the story.

Tar Beach was an instant—and enormous—success. Featuring the dream flights of Cassie Louise Lightfoot, *Tar Beach* was named a Caldecott Honor Book and won the Coretta Scott King Award for illustration.

To create *Tar Beach*, Faith drew upon her own childhood experiences—and added a healthy dose of imagination. She remembered how, for her apartment-dwelling family, going up on the black asphalt roof had been as much fun as going to the beach. Faith recalls, "My father would come home from work and take the mattress up for us, my mother would fix our bed and all of us kids would get a chance to sleep together on the one mattress." During those times, refreshed by cool breezes and stirred by the glorious vision of the city at night, Faith was filled with a magical feeling. "When you got up on the roof," Faith says, "you could see everything. The whole world was open to you. It was just totally special."

Tar Beach is a story of hope. Cassie's imagination lifts her up and takes her "flying among the stars." In the book she says, "Anyone can fly. All you need is somewhere to go that you can't get to any other way."

> ## DO IT YOURSELF!
> Can you fly? Faith Ringgold says you can—all you need is a little imagination! Sit down with a pen and paper and try to describe what it might feel like to fly. Where would you go? What would you see? Go on…close your eyes…and dream away.

AUTHOR

Joanne Ryder

BORN: September 16, 1946, in Lake Hiawatha, New Jersey
HOME: San Francisco, California

SELECTED TITLES

The Snail's Spell
1982

Inside Turtle's Shell, and Other Poems of the Field
1985

The Night Flight
1985

Chipmunk Song
1987

Step Into the Night
1988

White Bear, Ice Bear
1989

Lizard in the Sun
1990

Under Your Feet
1990

The Bear on the Moon
1991

When the Woods Hum
1991

Dancers in the Garden
1992

One Small Fish
1993

Sea Elf
1993

In many of Joanne Ryder's books about nature, readers are invited to let loose their imaginations. They are asked to become another creature—to creep on long padded toes like a lizard, to shake the snow from their fur like a great bear, to stuff acorns inside their furry cheeks like a chipmunk. The journey is always strange and exciting, filled with wonder and delight.

Yet in order for readers to take these imaginative journeys, Joanne has to do a lot of homework. "To write these stories," Joanne says, "I have to learn about an animal and imagine what it would feel like to live as the animal in its world. This is like a puzzle and a game for me, and I enjoy thinking it out."

Joanne strives to combine the imagination of a poet with the factual observations of a scientist. She says, "Often I need to observe an animal carefully before I write about it. I've had a great many pets—including rabbits, salamanders, ducks, pigeons, canaries, hamsters, fish, and snails—and some of them have found their way into my books."

EXPLORING HER WORLD

As a child growing up in Lake Hiawatha, New Jersey, and Brooklyn, New York, Joanne loved playing outdoors. In Lake Hiawatha, where Joanne lived for her first five years, there were always animals to encounter. Joanne fondly recalls, "It was a wonderful place to explore, full of treasures to discover. There were

just a few houses on our street, but there were woods all around, filled with small creatures."

A few years later, bustling Brooklyn offered a new world of discoveries. Joanne relates, "I tell children if they would like to imagine what I was like when I was six, they might read my book, *The Night Flight.* I was very much like Anna, the girl in the story. The dream Anna has of flying over the city was very much like my favorite dream. Every now and then, I still dream I can fly, and I always wake up feeling delighted."

Joanne's parents influenced her deeply. From her father, who was nicknamed "Bugs," Joanne learned to appreciate and try to understand nature. She warmly remembers, "My father liked to pick things up and examine them. He was the one who introduced me to nature up close. He would hold little creatures in his hand and say, 'Joanne, I have something really fabulous to show you.' Then he would open his fingers and show me whatever it was he had found—a beetle, a snail, a fuzzy caterpillar. Then gently he would let me hold it, and I could feel it move, wiggle, or crawl as I held it in my hand. So I became very comfortable holding tiny animals."

From her mother, who loved sunsets and hummingbirds, Joanne inherited a more poetic sense of nature. Joanne says, "My mother would like to walk along the water and watch sunsets. She liked a much broader scope of nature, like the changing of the seasons. But the little, teeny, weeny, squiggly things with lots of legs—those were not her cup of tea! She belonged to the 'squish' school. Her theory was, if you see a bug, squish it!"

Part scientist, part poet, Joanne absorbed the lessons of her parents. She looks to nature for pleasure and enjoyment. And often, she finds something more: "Going for a walk instantly calms me down," Joanne says. "It gives me a peaceful feeling. My problems often seem insignificant when I observe the natural world and witness its cycles. There's so much to discover—whether it's a flock of geese overhead or the fat, round moon rising in the sky once again."

Joanne believes the natural world is even more wonderful when you begin to unlock its secrets. This is the job of the scientist. "Science is all around us," Joanne firmly states. "We *are* science. Our bodies are science. We shouldn't be so afraid of that word, because so much of science is fascinating. It brings us closer to our world.

"Kids sometimes ask how many books I can write in a day," says Joanne, with a friendly laugh. "I wish it were that easy! My books are fairly short in length, yet it can take me a long time to write one. I have written a book in as short as an evening and as long as five years."

It's hard for many readers to understand the time that goes into writing a book. Joanne says, "When you look at the artwork, you can *see* the time that's put into it. But you can't see the time that goes into writing the 500 words in a picture book. You figure it probably took a very short amount of time. You don't realize that what you read is only the tip of the iceberg—and the rest of the iceberg is all the research and the many drafts that didn't make it."

Joanne loves her life as a writer. It is full of hard work. And if some of that work is fun, all the better! Joanne tells this story: "When I see kids, I ask them, 'What do you think I do as a writer?' They say that I sit at a desk and write. I show them a photograph of me walking in Golden Gate Park and say, 'This is me hard at work!' A writer can be working even when he or she is outside looking at a tree. There are so many things around you that can trigger your imagination and fill your mind with images and words."

THE SNAIL'S SPELL
by Joanne Ryder • Pictures by Lynne Cherry
OUTSTANDING SCIENCE BOOK FOR YOUNG CHILDREN
NEW YORK ACADEMY OF SCIENCES

SCHOLASTIC

"Ideas are like butterflies; you have to catch them quickly and carefully or they will escape and you may lose them forever."

DO IT YOURSELF!

Joanne Ryder says, "I just got a batch of stories from kids who modeled their stories after my Just-For-A-Day books (*Winter Whale*; *Sea Elf*; *Lizard in the Sun*; *White Bear, Ice Bear*). They became endangered animals for a day. They were really neat stories." Give it a try! Remember, like Joanne, you'll have to choose an animal, learn facts about that animal, and try to imagine what it feels like to be that animal. Have fun!

Allen Say

BORN: August 28, 1937, in Yokohama, Japan
HOME: San Francisco, California

SELECTED TITLES

The Bicycle Man
1982

How My Parents Learned to Eat
1984

The Boy of the Three-Year Nap
1988

A River Dream
1988

The Lost Lake
1989

El Chino
1990

Tree of Cranes
1991

———◇———

Growing up in Japan during World War II would have been hard for any child. For Allen Say, a shy, unathletic child, it was especially difficult. "I was a very sickly child," says Allen Say, perhaps with a slight trace of sadness at the memory. "My mother tells me that I suffered from every childhood disease known to medicine. I was a weakling, really."

Because of the war, Allen and his family were forced to move often, especially when the fighting came to mainland Japan. This constant moving about—always changing homes and attending new schools—made it hard for Allen to feel safe and secure. "I was terrified of schools and teachers," Allen admits. "That's what happens when you go to seven different grade schools. I was made to fight bullies at every school. So I escaped into reading and drawing.

"The marvelous thing that happened to me was that during recess I would draw. Students would stand behind me and watch. That's probably the first time I discovered that I had this power—it was the only power I had."

Though Allen was obviously a talented artist, Allen's father had different ambitions for his son. He wanted Allen to become a businessman. Allen recalls, "My parents were horrified. This was a disaster, to have their number one son turning into an artist. They tried everything to discourage me. I rebelled, of course; I drew."

After the war, normal life slowly returned to Japan. For the first time in years, Allen's family settled down in one place. But a new difficulty soon arose: his parents divorced. "It was a very traumatic experience for me," Allen confides.

Allen was sent to live with his father's mother, a strict disciplinarian. "We didn't like each other," Allen admits. "She didn't want to have me there and I didn't want to be there." Soon, a deal was reached: Allen's grandmother gave him the money to find another place to live. Each month she handed him an envelope filled with money, with which he would pay his rent and buy his food and anything else he needed. By age 12, Allen Say had his own apartment.

Suddenly, life took a dramatic turn for the better. Allen fulfilled a dream—he got hired as a cartoonist's apprentice. He recalls, "I had always wanted to become a cartoonist, so I went out and looked for my favorite, Noro Shinpei, one of the most famous cartoonists in Japan. I begged him to take me on as his student."

Working after school and on weekends, Allen drew four hours every day, helping out on the great master's comic strips. Allen found time for schoolwork late at night. After all, Allen could stay up as late as he liked—there was no one around to tell him when to go to bed.

> **"The father I talked about in _The Lost Lake_ was me. It was probably my way of saying I'm sorry to my own daughter because I wasn't spending enough time with her."**

Allen realizes how lucky he was to find a mentor, a person who could help him become a better artist and a better person. To this very day, Allen and Noro Shinpei are still friends. Allen says, "What I really learned from this man was how an artist thought and how he looked at life and how he lived his life, which was more important than learning how to draw.

"Those four years were the happiest of my life. Every time I finish a book, I send him a copy. I call him frequently. I can't tell you how comforting it is for me to have a master at my age. He sends me back report cards: 'Color: A. Composition: A.' That kind of thing. After I sent him _Tree of Cranes_, he wrote back and said: 'Not only have you become a master, but poetry has entered your work.'" Allen adds proudly, "What more can you ask?"

MOVING TO CALIFORNIA

Eventually, Allen's father resettled in California and sent for Allen to come live with him. It was a challenging experience. Allen was faced with a new country with new ways. Allen says, "I didn't speak any English at all. I said to myself, 'Where am I? What is this?'"

Gradually, Allen grew to like life in the United States. At the same time, a new interest arose: photography. After school, Allen gave up his dream of becoming an artist and instead began a career as a photographer. Still, he dabbled from time to time with watercolors and pen and ink.

"My first book was done in my photo studio," Allen remarks. "I began to draw and a story came out. I sent it out to various publishers. On my third try, Harper and Row took it. It was called _Dr. Smith's Safari._" But even with this success—and the success of later books—Allen didn't take children's books seriously. For him, it was only a hobby, something he did between photo assignments.

One day Allen reluctantly accepted a job to illustrate a manuscript called _The Boy of the Three-Year Nap._ Allen decided to do one last children's book and then call it quits. "But a strange thing happened," Allen remembers. "I started painting the pictures and I went back to my boyhood—into my master's studio—and all the memories came back to me. I said, 'I really like doing this.' I remembered all the joys of painting." That was the turning point. Allen Say had finally, at long last, found his joy. No small thing, indeed. From then on, Allen dedicated himself to writing and illustrating children's books.

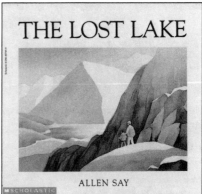

THE LOST LAKE

ALLEN SAY

SCHOLASTIC

DO IT YOURSELF!

Allen Say tells us: "All good artists have an excellent memory. You have to remember. You cannot imagine without memory. The great writer James Joyce said, 'The imagination is memory.' So that's my advice: Remember." Write a short story or draw a picture based upon one of your own childhood memories. If, like Allen, you'd like to change a detail or two, go right ahead. That's part of the fun!

Marjorie Weinman Sharmat

BORN: November 12, 1928, in Portland, Maine
HOME: Tucson, Arizona

SELECTED TITLES

Getting Something on Maggie Marmelstein
1971

Nate the Great
1972

Maggie Marmelstein for President
1975

Mooch the Messy
1976

I'm Terrific
1977

The 329th Friend
1979

Gila Monsters Meet You at the Airport
1980

Olivia Sharp, Agent for Secrets series
(with Mitchell Sharmat)
1989-1990

I'm the Best!
1991

◇

"My earliest ambition," admits author Marjorie Weinman Sharmat, "was to become a writer or a detective or a lion tamer.

"I began writing when I was eight. A friend and I published a newspaper called *The Snooper's Gazette* that we filled with news we obtained by spying on grown-ups for our detective agency. It achieved a circulation of about four—her parents and mine."

Marjorie's lifelong fascination with detective work led her to create one of the most beloved characters in contemporary children's literature—the hard-boiled private eye, Nate the Great, who is ably assisted by his loyal mutt, Sludge.

For Marjorie, it was love at first write: "I loved Nate from the very beginning," she says. "I knew that I wanted to write more books about Nate." Inspired, in part, by the deadpan dialogue of the *Dragnet* television series, Nate is a tough-talking sleuth with a nose for intrigue and a stomach for pancakes. Thanks to his dogged determination and unconventional brand of logic, Nate is still solving mysteries—21 years after his first case.

It's a challenge for Marjorie to keep coming up with new mysteries for Nate. She works hard to make each book different, while remaining true to the basic approach that readers have come to expect. Marjorie explains, "Increasingly, I've found that I've been working backward on my Nate cases. I look for something unusual but plausible for the ending and then I create a case leading up to it. Fortunately, the characterizations and dialogue always fall into place easily, and the twists and turns of plot arise from knowing where I'm going and trying to keep readers from finding out too soon."

Fortunately, Marjorie has had plenty of help over the years from her family. First and foremost, there's her husband, Mitchell Sharmat. While other authors must contend with the turmoil of writer's block, Marjorie has her own unique solution close at hand—she simply hollers, "Help!"

"If I run into a problem," Marjorie confides, "I just ask my husband. In fact, my husband came up with the solution to the first Nate book. He helped me with so many books over the years, I finally encouraged him to write his own." Marjorie adds with pride: "One of Mitch's titles, *Gregory, the Terrible Eater*, is the most successful book to come out of this household. I take great joy in his success."

Marjorie also credits her two sons, Craig and Andrew, for inspiring many episodes in her books. Andrew's own writing career was launched with his picture book, *Smedge*, inspired by the Sharmat's first dog, Fritz Melvin. Craig, who is a musician, co-wrote *Nate the Great and the Musical Note*. Marjorie's sister Rosalind suggested the premise and title for *Nate the Great and the Pillowcase*, and eventually became its coauthor.

> **"I like to write funny books because I think that life is basically a serious business and needs a humorous counterbalance."**

Like most of her ideas, the concept for *Gila Monsters Meet You at the Airport* stemmed directly from a personal experience. After living in New York, the Sharmat family decided to try the warmer climate of Tucson, Arizona. Marjorie remembers, "Before leaving, Andrew was warned by his friends about the strange things he would find out West, and when he arrived here, he discovered that his new western friends had rather wild ideas of what the East was like. Out of all this came *Gila Monsters Meet You at the Airport*—a definite possibility if you're an imaginative boy moving to the West!"

SHY AND INTROSPECTIVE
Marjorie was born and grew up in Portland, Maine. "I was introspective, nearsighted, and shy," she says, "and I still am. I was the stereotype. The glasses, staying indoors, and really loving books. I had friends, but there was a part of me that was reserved from the outside world. I just seemed

to communicate better with characters in books."

Reading Marjorie's books, it becomes clear that she brings a unique sensitivity to her work. She writes with compassion and understanding, and always roots for the underdog. "Loneliness is a theme which, perhaps above all others, appeals to me as a writer," Marjorie reveals. "I feel for people who are not one of the gang."

Most of Marjorie's writing begins with an idea for a character. Whether shy like Vanessa (*Say Hello, Vanessa*), egocentric like Jason Everett Bear (*I'm Terrific*), or simply irrepressible like Maggie Marmelstein, all of them seem to share one trait: "They boss me around," Marjorie complains with a laugh. "They tell me what they want to do. And I sort of feverishly try to keep up with them!"

Marjorie loves her life as a writer. "I'm glad things turned out the way they did," she says. She only regrets one thing: "The more books I publish, the less time I have to write. After the books are published, their business side starts to take over. Details, obligations, *more* work. As a result, Marjorie has been forced to stop visiting schools and giving speeches. And, most sadly, she can no longer answer the overwhelming number of letters she receives from children. "In the end," Marjorie says, "you can't go out and visit every classroom and answer every letter. I've decided that the best way for me to reach children is by writing my books. I'm grateful that there's someone there to read them."

DO IT YOURSELF!
Write your own mystery involving a detective. But first, listen to Marjorie's advice: "A lot of my Nate books are based on things that have happened to me. As a writer, I try to be alert. If something interesting occurs, I'll always ask myself, 'Could this happen to Nate?'" Marjorie adds one more tip: "A mystery needs a satisfying solution, so try to think of a solution before you start the story."

Peter Sis

BORN: May 11, 1949, in Brno, Moravia, Czechoslovakia
HOME: New York, New York

SELECTED TITLES

Rainbow Rhino
1987

Waving
1988

Going Up!
1989

Beach Ball
1990

Follow the Dream
1991

An Ocean World
1992

The Dragons Are Singing Tonight
1993

Komodo!
1993

Growing up in Czechoslovakia, behind the iron curtain, young Peter Sis often found himself daydreaming about distant lands and the wild adventures of bold explorers, like those who populate the stories of Jules Verne.

Czechoslovakia, in the 1950s and 1960s, was a land ruled by the strong hand of the Soviet government. Citizens had limited political and cultural freedoms. Travel beyond the iron curtain—the invisible border that separated the Western world from the Communist world—was simply not allowed for most citizens. Yet this is the environment in which Peter grew up to become a dreamer, artist, and explorer.

Peter, who now lives in New York with his wife and daughter, explains: "People can't choose if they live in a time of war or peace. It's amazing, though, that even within that very undesirable world we had time to play our games and have fun as children always do. In retrospect, I think I had a wonderful childhood, mostly thanks to my parents."

Peter is grateful to have grown up in an artistic household. His father, Vladimir, was a filmmaker and explorer. Alena, his mother, was an artist. They encouraged Peter to pursue his art and his dreams.

Because of his special status as a filmmaker, Peter's father was given the rare opportunity to travel outside the iron curtain. Peter recalls how his father, through countless stories, opened Peter's imagination to the possibilities of the world beyond his day-to-day experiences. "I would sit in the kitchen," Peter relates, "and he would describe things that I would never otherwise have been able to comprehend."

Though his parents warned him that an artist's life can be lonely and demanding, Peter felt certain that it was the life he wanted. Formal art school, however, provided a rude awakening. He was then in his early teens, and he soon became frustrated with the school's rules and restrictions. He explains, "The teachers wanted us to draw absolutely according to the style of the 19th century. It was very hard because there was really no space for fantasy or individuality."

Yet Peter persevered and graduated with a solid foundation of technical skill to complement his rich imagination. And he also found a new love—film animation. "Film was my passport to the whole world," Peter says.

Indeed, it was his work as an animator and short-filmmaker that opened new doors for Peter. "The Czech government let me out to work on a Swiss television series, but the situation was getting more and more difficult," Peter explains. "All the money I earned would go to the film company or the government in Prague, and I would only get a small percentage of it. Most of all, I was never sure, each time I returned home, that they would ever let me out again."

> ### "The most enjoyable part of creating a book is doing the initial sketches, putting the book together—the thinking part."

More and more, Peter began to feel trapped in his own country. In 1982, Peter was allowed to journey to Los Angeles, California, to work on a film project linked with the 1984 Summer Olympic Games. Once again, politics intervened. The Soviet Union and its satellite nations suddenly pulled out of the Olympics. Peter remembers it well: "The Czech passport office said that I should return home. But I had just had enough," he explains, matter-of-factly. "I simply didn't go back."

FOLLOWING THE DREAM
Imagine the incredible change in Peter's life. Suddenly he was in Los Angeles, California, a city of palm trees, hot tubs, and movie stars. He says, "All of a sudden things were completely different from what I was used to in Europe. I felt displaced and strange."

It was a trying time for the struggling artist. "I just couldn't figure out how things worked. I was in Los Angeles showing my work to people from the galleries who commission art, and they kept saying, 'It's too European, it's too dark. You have to lighten the sky and come up with some bright colors and some people on roller skates.' I was confused by it all."

Fortunately, Peter finally got a break. At a friend's suggestion, he sent a sample of his work to the children's book author Maurice Sendak. Impressed with Peter's work, Maurice called Peter and eventually introduced him to the art director of Greenwillow Books, Ava Weiss. She offered Peter a job immediately. His life as a children's book illustrator had begun.

Peter moved to New York, the center of publishing in the United States. Under the spell of new sights and impressions, he absorbed the vibrant life of New York's streets and people. Slowly, he got more and more work. Peter sold illustrations to magazines such as *The New York Times Book Review* and *The Atlantic Monthly*. And he created books—remarkable books full of magic and wonder.

One of Peter's most personal books is *Follow the Dream*, his artistic interpretation of Columbus's discovery of the new world. A book of stunning beauty and insight, *Follow the Dream* was inspired by Peter's own discovery of a new world. Peter wrote: "Columbus didn't let the walls hold him back. For him, the outside world was not to be feared but *explored*. And so he followed his dream."

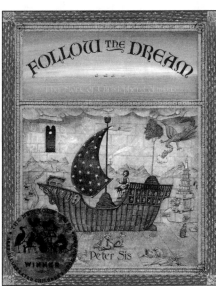

> ## DO IT YOURSELF!
> Peter's parents used to give him assignments. They would suggest a concept, and after a few weeks of thinking about it, Peter would have to produce an illustration based on that idea. Try it yourself. Think about Peter's life—think about walls, freedom, and being a poor artist from Europe suddenly finding yourself in Los Angeles or New York. Now draw a picture—it can be any picture you want—based on those impressions. Remember, as Peter says, "Anything goes!"

Lane Smith

BORN: August 25, 1959, in Tulsa, Oklahoma
HOME: New York, New York

SELECTED TITLES

Halloween ABC
1987

**The True Story
of the
Three Little Pigs!**
1989

The Big Pets
1991

**Glasses—
Who Needs 'Em?**
1991

**Time Warp Trio:
Knights of the
Kitchen Table**
1991

**Time Warp Trio:
The Not-So-Jolly
Roger**
1991

**The Stinky Cheese
Man and Other
Fairly Stupid Tales**
(Caldecott Honor Book)
1992

**The Happy Hocky
Family**
1993

———◇———

Although Lane Smith had already published two children's books, it wasn't until *The True Story of the Three Little Pigs!* that people really began to take him seriously. Well, not exactly seriously, but at least people did start to notice him. That's when most readers began to realize that Lane Smith was, well...*different.*

Lane remembers touring schools with Jon Scieszka (sounds like Fresca) to promote the *Three Little Pigs.* Visiting schools was a new experience for Lane. He recalls, "My problem was that I would get in there and the kids would start throwing stuff around and acting stupid. I didn't know how else to get them to be quiet so I'd throw something at them and be just as goofy. It's hard for me to be a serious authority figure. Someone will yell out, 'Hey, can you draw Bart Simpson with a hatchet in his head?' and I'll say, 'Okay! Got any colored markers?'"

The visits were fun-filled and riotous. Jon would read some of his new stories (which later became *The Stinky Cheese Man and Other Fairly Stupid Tales*) and Lane would draw along as he read. "I felt like Zippy the Drawing Chimp," Lane recalls with a laugh. "Jon would be reading and I'd be frantically trying to catch up with my drawings. I felt like I should be wearing a clown suit, making balloon animals. But actually, it's helpful to visit classrooms and see what kids respond to. You say the word 'stinky' and they're rolling on the floor."

A NICE, QUIET KID

For the first three years of his life, Lane lived in Tulsa, Oklahoma. Then his family moved to Corona, California. By all accounts, Lane enjoyed a typical childhood. Lane offers, "I was always drawing. And I was always writing little stories and odd things. I wasn't very social. I think that's why I decided on art as a career—it's such a nice, solitary thing to do. You can be by yourself and sit in a room and come up with all these goofy ideas."

Each summer Lane and his family would drive back to Oklahoma to visit relatives and friends. That's when Lane's love of popular culture began. "We'd take the old route 66," Lane fondly recalls. "We'd see the classic, kitschy America—Stucky gas stations, giant donut stands, concrete tipi motels—and I think that was a great influence on my work.

"When I was in art school I worked at Disneyland as a sweeper, except they called it a 'custodial host.' I think some of my artist friends were appalled that I was working at such a crassly commercial plastic place as Disneyland." Lane hesitates as he adds without a trace of apology: "But...I...love that stuff!"

These are some the things that influence Lane's art: old Monty Python television shows, comic books, Disney movies, Las Vegas, ugly shirts, *Mad* magazine, Buster Keaton, tacky wallpaper, European illustration, and anything else that makes his eyes light up. "My style is just a combination of everything I've put into my brain over the years—Paul Klee and Buster Keaton and Tex Avery—all this stuff mixes up and hopefully comes out in my own style."

"There are so many serious books out there and lots of people who do them really well. But there aren't many people who do really goofy work. It's so refreshing to see kids respond to funny stuff."

◇

Today Lane works in his new studio in Manhattan, not far from his home. Lane is a determined, if somewhat sporadic worker. "I like to take breaks," he admits. "I might take a break to watch cartoons, but it will sort of inspire me. Or I might sit down—I usually surround myself with all sorts of kids' books and stuff—and just read some James Marshall for half an hour. When I go back to my work, I can see it fresh again. The breaks help."

Lane is particularly excited about *The Happy Hocky Family*, which he describes as "a collection of short, quirky stories about a semi-normal American family."

Lane offers an example: "There's one about Holly Hocky, who has an ant farm. It's a story about responsibility. She says something like, 'Today is a hot day, and my ants have no windows in their ant farm. How can I help my ants? Oh, I know how. Silly me.' Then you turn the page and she's removed the roof of the ant farm so the ants can breathe. That's the end of the story. Then you turn the page again and the next story is about the new kitchen, but the page is just *crawling* with millions of ants!" Lane laughs again, then adds, "Maybe you need to see the illustrations to really understand it."

In 1992, Lane Smith won a Caldecott Honor for *The Stinky Cheese Man*. Lane says, "It is the book that I am the most pleased with from beginning to end. The stories work on their own; it works as a whole; and its transitional elements give it a film-like quality. It has running gags. It's completely resolved at the end. And," he says, saving the best for last, "it's really fun."

Nevertheless, winning such a prestigious award came as quite a surprise. "Traditionally, humor books haven't been taken very seriously. And even though people seem to like the book," he confesses, "it *is* kind of gross in parts. The stories are zany and the humor is sort of over the top; we have eyeballs bugging out and all that. So it was a total shock when teachers and librarians said they liked it. I was really honored."

Peter Spier

Born: June 6, 1927, in Amsterdam, Netherlands
Home: Shoreham, New York

SELECTED TITLES

The Fox Went Out on a Chilly Night
(Caldecott Honor Book)
1961

London Bridge Is Falling Down
1967

To Market! To Market!
1967

The Erie Canal
1970

The Star-Spangled Banner
1973

Tin-Lizzie
1975

Noah's Ark
(Caldecott Medal)
1977

Bored—Nothing to Do
1978

The Legend of New Amsterdam
1979

People
1980

Rain
1982

The Book of Jonah
1985

Father, May I Come?
1992

One fine afternoon in New England, Peter Spier and his wife Kay drove through the rolling landscape of the Berkshire mountains admiring the leaves on the trees, which had turned a beautiful array of crimson reds, sun yellows, and burnished golds. Their hearts were light and together they sang a favorite old folksong: "*The fox went out on a chilly night, and he prayed to the moon to give him light, for he'd many miles to go that night before he reached the town-o, town-o, town-o.*"

Suddenly struck with a new idea, Peter turned to Kay and asked, "Hey, wouldn't this area be a great setting for a picture book about that song?" Peter returned the next week, sketchbook in hand. He traveled throughout New England and sketched old houses, broken-down barns, chicken coops, farming tools, covered bridges, and more. From these sketches and observations, Peter created his award-winning book, *The Fox Went Out on a Chilly Night.*

Peter often takes to the road when he is creating a book. "If I have to draw someplace and I don't know what it looks like," Peter says, "I'll go there with a sketchbook in my hand. If it's a city, for example, I'll check into a hotel and roam the streets for the next week. I'll sketch, observe, and make notes. And if I had to draw a picture of pigs, I'd go to a farm and draw real pigs." Peter adds with conviction, "That's how you learn to draw. If you don't know what it looks like, don't draw it."

A disciplined worker, Peter laughs when people suggest that artists have an easy job. Mindful of deadlines—the date promised to the publisher that the book will be finished—Peter will labor all hours of the night to get the job done.

When he's completed a book, Peter smiles with the satisfaction that comes with all creative work, whether it be writing, carpentry, or sewing. "After I've finished," Peter explains, "I can look at it and say, 'If I hadn't sat in that chair for six months, it would never have existed.' It's a great feeling."

GROWING UP IN HOLLAND

As a child, Peter always had a good excuse if he was late for school. Peter grew up in a small Dutch village named Broek-in-Waterland. But to go to school, he had to travel into the city of Amsterdam. Peter recalls the trip: "My brother, sister, and I would walk from our house to the tram, and during the winter, skate. The tram was an ancient swaying vehicle filled with the smoke of cigars and clay pipes, and with fishermen from the village of Volendam who wore huge wooden shoes and baggy pants. They were taking their catch to market—herring and smoked eel were stacked in baskets in the aisles. An unforgettable aroma! After the tram ride, we took a ferry across the river. How I loved to be on the water in the early morning! Then back on another tram and a short walk to our school."

Peter's father, Joseph E.A. Spier, was a famous political cartoonist and journalist. Peter says that he owes a great deal of his drawing style to his father. "He was a great illustrator," Peter warmly recalls. "If you looked at his pictures next to mine, you'd see a great similarity—except that he drew *much* better than I do."

At the age of 25, after college and a three-year stint in the Royal Dutch Navy, Peter was offered work in the United States at a Dutch publishing company. Peter took the job, came to America, and has lived here ever since.

Acclaimed for his vivid panoramas, historical accuracy, and abundantly detailed work, Peter is one of the most respected artists in children's literature. His pictures are always full of activity, vitality, and humor. But equally important, Peter's books are expertly designed. Just as the words in a poem can create a pleasing rhythm, the variety in Peter's illustrations provides a welcome ebb and flow.

In Peter's remarkable book *Rain*, you can see how he balances many small pictures with dramatic, two-page spreads. Peter feels that these spreads provide places for the reader to rest, offering a space for thinking new thoughts. Peter cites a different example from his Caldecott Medal winner, *Noah's Ark*: "On one spread you'll see a small picture of Noah picking the eggs and other pictures of the little things he must have done. But these details don't justify a full-page picture. They aren't important enough. Or look at the picture of the elephant standing on the mouse's tail—I do it to change the pace, to break the somberness, to give the book rhythm and something humorous."

One of the most dramatic moments in any of Peter's books is a spread in *Noah's Ark*. On the left-hand page is a large picture of all the animals that didn't make it aboard the ark; left out in the cold, driving rain, they wait outside the closed doors of the ark in confusion. On the right-hand page, Peter provides two horizontal pictures. In the first, the animals are waist-deep in water. In the next picture, only the ark is seen—off in the far distance, buffeted by waves, alone.

At an age when most people have retired from their jobs, Peter Spier still has book projects on the back burner. And why not? Peter says, "As long as your hand is steady, you can keep on making books for as long as you wish. The wonderful thing for me, at this stage of my life, is that I don't *have* to do it anymore. I'm doing it because it's still fun."

NOAH'S ARK

Illustrated by PETER SPIER

> "When I wrote *People*, I was thinking that instead of holding our differences against each other, wouldn't it be better to be grateful for them and to rejoice in them."

DO IT YOURSELF!

How did Peter Spier learn to draw so well? He gives one word:"Practice!" He also stresses the importance of drawing from real life. Peter, who often makes quick sketches of friends and neighbors, says, "Take a sketchbook outside and draw something. Once you capture a shape, it's yours forever. The same is true with writing. Stick to it, keep on doing it—and practice!"

Rosemary Wells

BORN: January 29, 1943, in New York, New York
HOME: Briarcliff Manor, New York

SELECTED TITLES

Benjamin and Tulip
1973

Noisy Nora
1973

Stanley and Rhoda
1978

When No One Was Looking
1980

Timothy Goes to School
1981

Hazel's Amazing Mother
1985

Max's Chocolate Chicken
1986

Through the Hidden Door
1987

Shy Charles
1988

Max's Dragon Shirt
1991

Voyage to the Bunny Planet
1992

◇

An intelligent, thoughtful woman who is fiercely dedicated to her craft, Rosemary Wells has written and illustrated more than 40 books for young children, in addition to six novels for teenagers. Her experience has provided her with a unique perspective on the art of writing: "All really significant work of any quality comes not because I feel that *I'm* doing it, but because it's coming to me."

The artist, in Rosemary's view, is a conduit through which inspiration flows. Still, she does not mean to suggest that a person can simply sit down and wait for great ideas to happen miraculously. Rosemary offers a comparison: "Look at a great athlete like Martina Navratilova. She never lets a day go by without playing tennis for two hours because she has to keep sharp. In order to become what she became, she had to play for hours and hours and hours, for years and years and years. It's true of all talents."

"None of this is easy," Rosemary is quick to admit. "To become a professional writer is very, very hard. But we *all* need to learn how to write to some extent—so writing's different. We don't all need to learn how to play the violin or even how to play tennis, but we all need to know how to write."

Though Rosemary is both a writer and an illustrator, she firmly believes that the story is the central part of a good picture book. "The misconception is that it is relatively easy to write for children, that illustrating is the hard part. I believe the opposite is true," she states. "The words come first. The story begins with feelings and is embellished with humor, adventure, and character. The words it takes to bring these elements to life are paramount. When they are truly well done the book becomes poetry."

According to Rosemary, writing for children is much more difficult than writing for adults. The main reason: A children's book must remain enjoyable even after it has been read aloud 500 times! Rosemary states, "Writing for young children is the rarest voice in all literature."

BEGINNING WITH EMOTIONS

To create her stories, Rosemary often draws upon episodes in her own life and the lives of her two daughters, Victoria and Meg. A little white terrier and his heirs also play important roles. Rosemary explains, "Our West Highland white terrier, Angus, had the shape and expressions to become Benjamin, Tulip, and Timothy, and all the other animals I have made up for my stories. He also appears as himself in a couple of books."

Although Rosemary will sometimes get an idea from observing her own children, she believes that "it's much more important to have been a child than to have children. It's because I was a child and I'm very close to that time in my life that I can do this. Incidents from childhood are universal."

While she stresses that each book has a logic of its own—"there is no single way of doing it"—Rosemary usually begins by focusing on one particular character. "The central issue in all my books is emotional content," she says. "I continually pick similar themes. One of the themes I use a lot is belonging to a group or feeling that you don't belong."

Like most writers, Rosemary takes small incidents—a snatch of overheard conversation, a long-held memory, an amusing thought—and runs them through to their logical conclusions in her mind.

Rosemary gives an example: "When Beezoo was in second grade, she wanted more than anything to take in her favorite stuffed animal for show and tell. She decided at the last minute against it, however, because, as she put it, 'The boys would rip it up.'" With that insight in mind, Rosemary wrote *Hazel's Amazing Mother*.

"The thing that fiction writers do, of course, is change everything," Rosemary confesses. "We don't write

things up as case histories. You change it, reduce it, or embellish it to make the story better.

"Three-quarters of all writing is revising," Rosemary says. "It's tremendously important to work hard, to practice, and to revise—to do things again and again and again until they are right. You can't just snap it out and say it's going to be right the first time. It isn't right," she says matter-of-factly, "until it's right.

"When I go to workshops for young writers, I bring a kaleidoscope with a detachable end, but I don't tell them it's a kaleidoscope at first," Rosemary explains. "Then I show them a handful of junk—paper clips, little plastic files, a couple of buttons—the kind of stuff you might find at the bottom of a drawer and throw out. I tell them that when you put all these different shapes and colors into the kaleidoscope, and you hold it up to your eyes, you make a rose window."

Rosemary pauses a moment before making her point: "Everybody makes a different window," she says. "You turn the kaleidoscope and the exact image can never be repeated again. The design is yours to make from the ordinary essence of life. That's what writing is about. Very ordinary things become a rose window if you organize them and you let yourself think about it. Without writing, without writing *well*, we cannot convey many ideas. And without ideas," Rosemary concludes, "we become drones."

NOISY NORA

Story and pictures by
ROSEMARY WELLS

SCHOLASTIC

Hans Wilhelm

BORN: September 21, 1945, in Bremen, Germany
HOME: Westport, Connecticut

SELECTED TITLES

Tales From the Land Under My Table
1983

Bunny Trouble
1985

I'll Always Love You
1985

Let's Be Friends Again!
1986

Oh, What a Mess
1988

Tyrone the Horrible
1988

Friends Are Forever
1989

A Cool Kid Like Me
1990

Tyrone the Double Dirty Rotten Cheater
1990

The Bremen Town Musicians
1992

The Boy Who Wasn't There
1993

—————◇—————

When we hear the advice, "Write about what you know," most of us think in terms of place or events. We think of wild roller coaster rides or funny incidents that happened in school. Hans Wilhelm, author and illustrator of more than 100 books for children, might change that advice to "Write about what you feel." That's because Hans believes a book is basically a sharing of emotions. "Just as a letter is a very personal thing," Hans explains, "so is a book."

Hans describes how the creative process works for him: "The basic emotion in the book must be something that is also in me. So I must come in touch with that problem. I don't believe there are solely childhood problems. The fear of rejection, loneliness, sibling rivalry, dealing with a bully—you don't outgrow these things as an adult. I think all of our feelings are the same."

One of Hans's most famous books, *I'll Always Love You,* illustrates his point about the role of emotion in writing. It is the story of a friendship between a young boy and his dog, Elfie. With charming, often humorous pictures and very few words, Hans shows how the boy and the dog grow up together. As the boy gets bigger and stronger, the dog grows older and weaker. Eventually, as would happen in real life, Elfie dies.

Hans confesses, *"I'll Always Love You* is autobiographical. The dog in my life was called Elfie. I wrote that book years later, long after Elfie died."

In order to write the book, Hans had to remember his childhood feelings. The love he felt, and the sadness he endured. Readers don't have to own a dog to appreciate the story, however. It is about a universal feeling that everyone encounters at one time or another. Hans says, "I think that book relates not only to animals, but to human beings as well. It could be about losing a parent or a friend. I think readers sense this."

Hans offers this advice to young writers and illustrators: "You cannot be afraid of showing your true self if you wish to become an author or illustrator of books. Each page and each word can reveal your emotions and fears."

REAL EMOTIONS AND BELLY LAUGHS, TOO!

A soccer-loving bunny, a clumsy cow, a bully dinosaur, a pig who hates a mess—Hans always adds at least a touch of humor to each of his books.

He says, "Humor is very important for me in most of my books. The funny side is really a way of saying hello to the reader. It says, 'Come on, I'll take you to a magical land and we'll have a good time together.'"

Hans Wilhelm sits down at his table and begins the workday bright and early. He says, "I am a morning person, so that's the best time for me to have creative ideas and thoughts. Therefore, I write and illustrate in the morning and use the afternoon for the administrative part of my work." Hans usually works in his studio in Connecticut, but he also has another studio in his native Germany.

"I think that a children's book is an adult book that is so good it even satisfies children."

Hans believes that working on a story is a process of discovery. While writing and sketching, Hans tries to stay open to new ideas as they occur. "Once I see the characters on my sheet of paper, they begin to communicate with me and often they develop quite differently from what I originally had in mind. I always allow for fun and surprises as I work on a story."

Hans gets his ideas by using his imagination, his dreams, and things that happen in his own life. He also likes to listen. Just quietly listening, Hans tells us, is a wonderful way to discover ideas. "Many things we hear or read are so incredible that they make wonderful stories!"

An idea may suddenly come to him when he least expects it. Hans remembers, "The idea for *Bunny Trouble* came to me on a sunny afternoon when I was resting in my hammock and not thinking of anything in particular. Suddenly there

was a new idea in my head. Soon it became a whole story and I had to go inside to write it down and make my first sketches."

Hans grew up in Bremen, Germany. He recalls, "Some of my favorite memories are of climbing trees, building tree houses, and watching wild animals." As a child, Hans always wrote and illustrated his own stories just for fun.

When Hans first came to the United States many years ago, he had to struggle with the English language. He thinks this made him work harder on his illustrations. "This struggle," Hans says, "forced me to express feelings, fine nuances, and subtleties in my illustrations. The visual does not have language barriers. In my pictures I can converse and say all the things that I wish to communicate." Hans points out, "The illustrations are a passport to everybody's heart, without any translations!"

With a warm blend of seriousness and zany humor, Hans Wilhelm's books have offered a good time to thousands of children in many different countries. For Hans, it's a dream come true. "I try to have a good time while I'm making a book," Hans confides. "Even if the process of making a book also means a lot of sweating, the overall experience must also be joyful and positive. I believe that making books is my way of sharing my joy with others."

DO IT YOURSELF!

Hans Wilhelm has said, "A book is basically nothing other than a letter, because it, too, is a sharing of emotions." Try to write a letter to a friend or a family member. In your letter, write about something— a person, a place, an event—that gave you a special feeling. The emotion could be anything: joy, fear, sadness, love. Then ask yourself, "Is there any way I could turn this letter into a story?"

Charlotte Zolotow

BORN: June 26, 1915, in Norfolk, Virginia
HOME: Hastings-on-Hudson, New York

As the author of more than 70 books for children, Charlotte Zolotow explores the ordinary emotions that touch a child's life. Yet her writing is anything but ordinary. With a keen ear for the sound of words and an artist's eye for detail, Charlotte Zolotow is a poet of the everyday—capturing the emotions that bring us together and the events that define our lives.

It is a great pleasure to listen to Charlotte's books read aloud. The flow of words seems to wash over the reader like soothing waves. Many of her books are like illustrated poems— quiet, reflective, heartfelt. Charlotte, who spends hours smoothing out the rhythm and balance of her sentences, is delighted to be called a poet. She responds cheerfully, "I love to hear that. I was talking to a group of third-graders the other day in a bookstore and one little girl asked, 'Why do some of your books sound like poetry?' I consider that a great compliment."

Charlotte's books are often based on her feelings or moods she may have experienced. Writing with sensitivity and grace, Charlotte explores the twists and turns of her own meandering heart. She recalls the comment of children's book editor Ursula Nordstrom, who said: "Everybody who writes children's books should have a direct line to their own childhood."

Charlotte explains, "All of my books are based on an adult emotion that connects with a similar emotion that I had as a child." The key to Charlotte's writing is in how well she can convey that emotion. Says Charlotte, "I like each of my books for a different reason, because each comes out of a different emotion. If a book succeeds in bringing an emotion into focus, then I like that book very much."

MISSING A FRIEND OR FATHER

For example, in the book *If You Listen* a young girl misses her father, who is away from home. Charlotte says that this feeling—missing an absent friend—is one she has experienced many times as an adult. Charlotte adds, "Also, as a child, my father traveled a lot and I was very fond of him. I can remember sitting there and thinking about him, knowing that somewhere, he was out there and he was coming back to me."

Now read this passage taken from *If You Listen*. Notice how Charlotte uses a detail, the bird, to fill the moment with feeling: "The little girl sat still a long time. She was thinking of her father. She looked up at the sky. It was a clear blue. One bird circled and circled overhead. She watched until he flew away."

As if going to a well and drawing up buckets of cool, fresh water, Charlotte is constantly drawing on her own experiences for inspiration. Charlotte grew up with a sister, Dorothy, who was six years older—so she wrote *Big Sister and Little Sister*. Charlotte's husband used to work upstairs as a writer—so she wrote *The Poodle Who Barked at the Wind*. Book after book, the facts of Charlotte's life slowly come out. To learn something about Charlotte today, read *I Know a Lady*. Charlotte says, "This is the first time in my life that I've been without a dog, but I live on a street where there are several. In fact, I've just been out with Matilda, who turns up in *I Know a Lady*; she comes over each morning for her dog biscuit."

> **"Things that matter to children—that's what I try to get into my books. Things that are very important, even if they aren't important to the adults around them."**

⬧

Charlotte, who worked as a children's book editor for many years, enjoys going on solitary walks by the Hudson River. This is her time—a chance to be quiet, to watch the world, to be refreshed by nature. Charlotte says, "You just let your mind go free and then out of it things fall into place."

Ideas, for Charlotte, come at times such as this. She may be overcome with a mood or an emotion. The stories, it seems, come from her heart, not her head. Charlotte tries to explain: "When you are washing dishes, or doing any manual task—when you are thinking that you are *not* thinking—that is the time when things really begin to take shape."

Like many writers, Charlotte begins by writing too much. In the beginning, she tries to capture the feeling. "Often with writing," says the thoughtful author, "you begin by writing too much. And out of it suddenly emerges one line that's exactly right. That one line reveals the essence of the story. It's a strange process that's almost impossible to describe."

During revision, Charlotte reads her manuscript out loud to hear how it sounds. Charlotte says, "I find that I might write pages of description—I love to write description—and then rereading it I see how I could set the mood in three sentences rather than three pages. So I do a great deal of cutting back." Almost with a sense of wonder, Charlotte adds, "With some manuscripts revision takes forever, while with others it just sort of happens... magically."

When speaking with Charlotte Zolotow, one idea comes up again and again: *Write from the heart*. Charlotte says, "I don't think children should be marked on spelling, or at least if they are marked it should be separate from content. When you try to teach someone how to write, what you should say is: 'Put down your thoughts. Put down the things that are hard to say, the things that you want to say.' Then, let that student be judged on the content, on how honest he or she is."

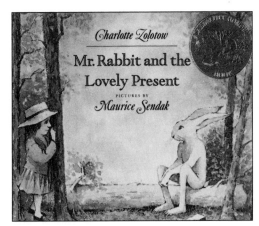

Charlotte Zolotow
Mr. Rabbit and the Lovely Present
PICTURES BY
Maurice Sendak

> ## DO IT YOURSELF!
> Charlotte recommends this simple writing exercise: "Write a line about feeling sad, mad, bad, or glad—something you really feel. Give examples of incidents that have made you feel that way. Some of these examples might make a good book or two!"

INTERMEDIATE BOOKS

AUTHORS AND ILLUSTRATORS

PREFACE

I f you are lucky, there is a special place where you go to be alone with a good book. It may be an overstuffed chair with a cozy blanket; it may be a pile of floor pillows stacked where the sun streams in late in the day; it may even be your bed. Whenever you go there to read, that comfortable spot is like a launching pad. From there, you can take off and visit places that stir your imagination. Each journey is piloted by an author, your partner in adventure.

Get ready to meet some talented writers, pilots of millions and millions of journeys. They are graced with storytelling ability; they live to share it. As Joyce Carol Thomas said, "What you write is a gift. You write the best you can write. That's the joy of it."

In the following profiles, 30 of your favorite authors will let you in on some of their secrets. As you meet them, perhaps you will marvel, as I do, at the connection that can exist between the writer in a workroom and the reader in a comfortable chair, spanning space and time. As Cynthia DeFelice told me, "I want to create the experience that I had when I was a kid reading books. I just jumped into the story."

Deborah Kovacs

Natalie Babbitt

BORN: July 28, 1932, in Dayton Ohio
HOME: Providence, Rhode Island

SELECTED TITLES

Phoebe's Revolt
1968

The Search for Delicious
1969

Kneeknock Rose
(Newbery Honor Book)
1970

The Something
1970

Goody Hall
1971

The Devil's Storybook
1974

Tuck Everlasting
1975

The Eyes of the Amaryllis
1977

Herbert Rowbarge
1982

The Devil's Other Storybook
1987

Nellie: A Cat on Her Own
1989

Many of Natalie Babbitt's books are fantasies set in the past because she thinks it's easier to believe a fantasy somehow if it is set 30 or 50 years ago. "Then it could really have happened," she says. "Not that you think it really did, but it just has more reality." She says she has trouble suspending her disbelief when she reads a fantasy with characters wearing contemporary clothes. "To me, blue jeans and sneakers don't mix with fantasy."

When writing about the past, Natalie tries to be accurate with details. For example, when she was writing *Eyes of the Amaryllis*, set in 19th-century Cape Cod, in which stormy weather and the timing of high tides play important parts, Natalie consulted tide charts from the time the story took place. She also did a lot of research about hurricanes. "I was very careful. It's worth it. There's always the chance that some meteorologist or some expert on weather will be reading the book to his kids. If you're careless, you get found out."

Natalie is mainly writing picture books these days, which she illustrates herself. She hasn't written a novel in 10 years. Why did she stop? "I've always drawn whatever pictures my novels have had," she explains, adding that she had originally intended to be primarily an illustrator. "I wanted to finish off my career in that direction," she says. "I wanted to find out what I could really do before I got too old to do it."

As a child, Natalie was shy and spent a lot of time by herself. "I drew all the time. I used to come home after school and set up little schedules for myself," she says. "For a two-week period, I would draw nothing but hands. Nobody thought it was strange at the time, but I suppose I do when I think of it now."

BEING SOMEBODY

Natalie came to her calling as a writer and illustrator because, she says, "I just wanted to be somebody. I always assumed I would be." She was raised in a "very matriarchal family," with a mother who instilled in her and her sister the belief that they could do it all—get married, have families, and have careers. Sadly, her mother died fairly soon after Natalie was married, and without her mother's strong support and encouragement, Natalie lost confidence in herself. For the next 10 years, she says, she was very frustrated, and in some ways very unhappy. It was the frustration, she believes, that drove her to pursue her career. "I had decided when I was nine that I wanted to be an illustrator," she says. "You can decide that, but it's something else to actually do it with nobody but yourself to depend on for moral support."

The first book she illustrated that was published, *The Forty-Ninth Magician*, was written by her husband, Sam. "That was logical," she says. "He was a terrific writer. He even won writing prizes in college." When they sold the book, they went to New York City to meet their editor, Michael di Capua. "That was an incredible moment," she says. "I cannot properly describe it. He liked the story, but what he was really interested in were the pictures. This was incredible to me. Incredible. I was very lucky to find him. Everything I do, I do for him. To me, he is the eye and the ear."

> ## "Most of the time the names of my characters are significant in ways the reader doesn't necessarily know about."

After the first book, Sam decided he didn't want to pursue that type of work, so Natalie started to write. She wrote and illustrated several picture books, then authored her first novel, *The Search for Delicious*. She was amazed at how much fun it was to write something long, "where there is a lot of elbow room." That book started out as a picture book. But the more Natalie worked on it, the more intricate it became. "It's a fairy tale, but it's a complicated story. I couldn't write such a complicated book today. No way."

Making the transition from illustrator to novelist was much harder than Natalie had expected. Still, she persisted. "I was too dumb to know how hard it was," she says. In fact, Natalie thinks most people have no idea how difficult writing is.

"Writing is hard, hard work," she says. "These stories do not spring full-blown into the writer's mind from some muse. Anybody who thinks that they do has a lot to learn."

Natalie has pictures in her mind when she writes, but she doesn't think that's because she started out as an illustrator. "To me, writing a novel is very much like creating a play," she says. "You cast it, you do the set, the lighting, and everything else."

When she sits down to create a story, Natalie often thinks back to the year she was in fifth grade, a year in her life she remembers fondly. "Fifth-graders today are the same way I was," she says. "That was a happy year for me. I remember everything about it. I remember all my friends and what I cared about and what we did. I try to write the kind of story that I would have liked then."

Though Natalie has done a lot of teaching, she really doesn't think it's possible to teach anyone to be a writer. "You can teach the mechanics. That's about it," she says. "Nobody can teach you to write a beautiful sentence. You've got to learn how to do that by reading ceaseless examples. Even bad stuff."

NATALIE BABBITT
Tuck Everlasting

DO IT YOURSELF!

Natalie is a big fan of puzzles and word games. There is a word game she thinks can help you develop your ear so you don't repeat words in your stories. Write sentences that include homonyms—words that sound alike but have different meanings, such as: In the fall, the leaves fall from the trees. Or: It's hard to plant flowers in the winter when the ground is hard. Then go back and rewrite the sentences to eliminate one of the homonyms.

Graeme Base

BORN: April 6, 1958, in Amershame, England
HOME: Melbourne, Australia

SELECTED TITLES

Animalia
1986

The Eleventh Hour: A Curious Mystery
1988

The Sign of the Seahorse
1992

◇

Artist and writer Graeme Base carries a sketchbook along when he knows he's going someplace that might be interesting. "I'm not saying I'm a boy scout who is prepared at all times," he admits. "Sometimes I see something interesting and I have to run to a store and buy a notebook."

A sketchbook was invaluable when he was creating *The Eleventh Hour*, an elaborate mystery story with luxurious, complicated illustrations. "I wanted to do a mystery story and hide all the clues," Graeme says. But that great idea wasn't developed until he embarked on a round-the-world trip with his wife, Robyn. "I used a sketchbook as we traveled. I also took a camera along. We started in Thailand, went to Northern India and Nepal, than we went down through Egypt and into Kenya and Tanzania and England and Europe."All the way around the world, he thought about the book. "If I saw a beautiful piece of architecture or an interesting artifact, I would say to myself, 'How can I use that in the book?'" Gradually, *The Eleventh Hour* became as much a record of that fabulous trip as it was a mystery story. "It was tremendously valuable that I went traveling just at that particular moment before doing the book. The final product was the result of traveling and seeing things and experiencing things."

Graeme couldn't use a sketchbook when working on his latest book, *The Sign of the Seahorse*, though, because the subject matter required that he do

his research underwater. That book came about as the result of a trip Graeme took to Martinique in the Caribbean, where he learned to scuba dive. Living in Australia, he had always spent lots of time by the sea, but he had never been scuba diving before. "I was blown away by what I saw underwater. I was amazed at how much I could see when I spent a good long time underwater, studying details."

DIVING IN

After that first experience diving, he decided to do a book about a coral reef. To do his research, he did some more diving at the Great Barrier Reef in Australia. There he gathered lots of information about coral reefs and different shapes and forms of coral. To Graeme, the environment of the coral reef is very similar to that of a tropical rainforest. Both are full of different, fascinating life forms, and both are dramatically endangered. "If you look at a rainforest closely, you'll realize that each tree is home to untold numbers of species—plants that grow within the boughs of the tree, rare orchids, insects, and birds that eat the insects."

When not drawing or traveling, Graeme enjoys music: listening to it, writing it, and performing it. "This comes from my childhood," he says. "Rather than having very strong memories of being read stories, I remember music being played." He recalls such works as *Carnival of the Animals* by Saint-Saëns and Prokofiev's *Peter and the Wolf* as being especially influential.

Growing up, Graeme thought of himself as an artist rather than a writer. "I never had any ambition to be a writer," he says. "I always enjoyed words, though, and I was good at grammar." He thinks that the most important thing that happened to him when he was a child was that he moved from England to Australia. There, says Graeme, "I broke free of the reins of staid British traditions, of 'what one does.' I was in a new country where it was exciting and open and you got the feeling you could have been the first person to stand somewhere, or to do something. That gave me a feeling of tremendous confidence."

Moving to Australia also opened Graeme's eyes to the world of wildlife. "It was great to come to a new country and discover a whole new line of beasties," he remembers. "My mum and dad were classic hedgerow British birdwatchers. They'd get us in the car and we'd go all over, to national parks and wildlife sanctuaries. After I'd lived in Australia a year, I knew more about its animals than my friends who had lived in Australia all their lives."

Combining his interest in wildlife with his skills as an artist came naturally to Graeme, even when he was still very young. Being able to draw well had another advantage, too. "Coming from England and going to

Australia, I found myself on the bottom of the social heap," he remembers. "I was a little English kid who couldn't speak properly. I didn't know the rules for Australian football. But I could draw pictures like nobody else in the class."

Graeme has never thought of himself as specifically a children's book author or illustrator. He just creates books about things that appeal to him. "I don't talk down or up to any particular age group," he says. "I don't try to inveigle somebody into my book to give a message. I do what strikes me. Whoever picks up the book can do with it what they like."

When asked if he has any advice for kids who hope to create books one day, Graeme says, "Sell the TV." He's serious. He also hopes that kids realize it's much more important to do what you want to do, than to try to do things that may make you a lot of money. "Go for ideas that are so fantastic you can't bear not to do them," he recommends.

Graeme is very happy with the way his work and his life blend together. "People ask me, 'Do you enjoy your work, combining adventures with art?' I answer, 'Look at me! I'm smiling!' Being able to be creative, to travel the world, to draw my fantasies—if anyone can think of a better job description, I want their phone number!"

"I always said, 'When I grow up I'm going to be an artist.'"

DO IT YOURSELF!

Graeme Base's *Eleventh Hour* was based on observations he made while on a trip. Test your powers of observation. For an entire day, carry a pocket-sized notebook with you. In the notebook, make a list, numbered 1 to 50. Write down 50 things that you observe during the course of a day. Then write a story based on five of those things.

Joan Blos

BORN: December 9, 1928, in New York, New York
HOME: Ann Arbor, Michigan

When Joan Blos writes a book of historical fiction, she enjoys doing the research most of all. Referring to it as "the treasure hunt" of the process, Joan says she has to tell herself to stop researching and to start writing. And even then, she's prone to slipping back to the library to find a specific fact. "I once spent a day and a half trying to find out when and how the state motto of Michigan was established," Joan laughs.

Joan faced one of her biggest challenges as a writer when she wrote the dialogue for *A Gathering of Days*, which is set in the 1830s. She says, "Of course, there are no tape recordings of people talking back then." Because she wanted her characters' speech to be as accurate as possible, she worked hard to develop her own sense of how language was used, especially among children, in that faraway time. "My sense of the language came from reading a variety of things written in the 19th century, like newspapers, letters, and reminiscences." She also listened to current New England speech. "I began to have a sense of its rhythm and its pacing. Once I hit on something that sounded right to me, it was easy to sustain the language. In the beginning, I thought it was going to be hard. But after a few pages, I just got used to it."

Joan's sense of the era's language also developed from studying 19th-century artifacts. "I spent hours looking at the tools they used, the clothes they wore, the furnishings in their houses. I began to feel that through that kind of study, as much as reading, I learned about the people of the time and how they might have thought and spoken."

At times, Joan becomes so in tune with the era she's writing about that eerie coincidences occur. "I tell kids that it's interesting to me and a little spooky that some things that I made up for the sake of the story turned out to be true," says Joan. "It comes from paying attention to what you're working with."

LEAVING SPACE FOR THE READERS

Joan is a hunt-and-peck typist who uses a computer "very badly." She revises "over and over and over." "Even with the computer," says Joan, "I still do the first draft with a pencil in one hand and an eraser in the other." When she really gets going, "I stop using the eraser and start crossing things out."

When Joan writes picture books, she is very conscious of pacing the text in a way that both respects and makes use of the format of the book. "I'm aware that I have to cut or split my idea into two parts that can go on two facing pages." To her, it doesn't matter if the final artwork looks the way she imagined it would. She likes to give the illustrator freedom to interpret the text and leave his or her unique stamp on the finished product.

"Occasionally something unexpected happens in the story I'm writing. Those moments are marvelous. Those moments keep me at it."

Similarly, Joan likes to "leave space for the readers," viewing them as her partners in the making of stories. Once she was telling a class about how she just did not describe things when she lacked information. "For example," she said, "I explained that despite all the research I had done for *A Gathering of Days,* I still didn't know what color houses were in the early 19th century in the particular part of New Hampshire where the story takes place. I just knew that at that time they weren't painted white. That is one of the advantages of the diary form. It spares you a lot of description!" But even before Joan finished explaining this, a girl at the back of the room waved her hand in agitation. "But you *did* say what color the house was," she insisted. "In fact, you said it was red!" Joan said she didn't think so, but the girl had sounded so positive, Joan went home and carefully looked through the book. Joan had been right. Nowhere had she written anything about the color of the house. "Clearly this girl had formed a

picture out of what I had offered, combined it with some experience or knowledge or assumptions of her own, and colored in the house. That was a striking demonstration of how very strongly a reader can feel."

Joan thinks of reading a novel or a picture book as a real experience that brings up real emotions. "When your protagonist is caught in a desperate situation, you feel truly anxious and don't want to stop reading until you know how everything turns out." Joan believes you can learn from a book the same way you learn from life. "Not only that, if you and I have both read the same book, we can talk about it together, like a shared experience," she says.

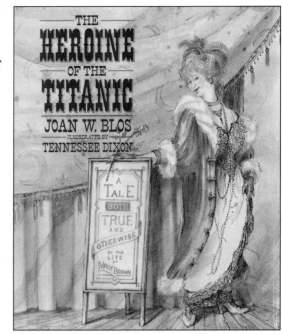

Eve Bunting

BORN: December 19, 1928, in Maghera, Northern Ireland
HOME: Pasadena, California

SELECTED TITLES

One More Flight
1976

The Big Red Barn
1979

Karen Kepplewhite Is the World's Best Kisser
1983

Face at the Edge of the World
1985

Sixth Grade Sleepover
1986

How Many Days to America?: A Thanksgiving Story
1988

A Sudden Silence
1988

The Ghost Children
1989

The Wednesday Surprise
1989

Such Nice Kids
1990

The Wall
1990

Fly Away Home
1991

◇

Eve Bunting, who is the author of more than 100 children's books, almost never became a writer at all. Growing up in Ireland, surrounded by books that she read and that were lovingly read to her by her father, she had always thought of herself as "good" at writing, and she had been encouraged all along the way by her teachers. Then she ran across an English teacher in college who failed to see her potential. "He flunked me," she recalls today. She can still remember how discouraged she felt. She abandoned all hope of becoming an English teacher at that time, and stopped thinking of herself as a writer for a number of years.

It wasn't until much later, after she was married, had children, and had moved to California, that Eve overcame this feeling. "I saw a class about writing in the catalogue of a local junior college," says Eve. "I remembered that I used to love to write. I told myself, 'I should just go.' It took quite a bit of push for me, since it had been a while." But go she did, and she loved it from the beginning. Twenty years later, she still hasn't stopped writing.

WRITING ON THE GO

Eve writes with a pencil and paper, which she finds very convenient because she can write wherever she happens to be. "Sometimes I'll amuse a group of kids I'm speaking to by showing them that I've written my first draft on the back of an airplane barf bag," she says. "I once wrote a

picture book on the back of an opera program, using a flashlight, while the opera was going on!"

As a writer, Eve is driven by words that "bubble up" within her. "I have to put them down. Thoughts have no scheduled time to start or stop." Some days, she doesn't write at all. "But I usually think about writing every day." Her husband tries to slow her down by saying, "Five days a week is enough for anybody." But, says Eve, "If I have an idea, I'll go for it."

Eve grew up in a tiny village in Northern Ireland. "I come from the Irish tradition of storytellers," she says. "My father read to me all the time." What he read was poetry, particularly long epic poems that he cherished, such as Longfellow's "Hiawatha."

"As he read," Eve remembers, "he would stop and say to me, 'Do you understand this, darlin'?' And I'd say, 'Yeah.' And he'd say, 'Tell me what is happening,' and I would." Her father also gave her books of her own to read, books she remembers fondly, such as *Anne of Green Gables, The Wind in the Willows, Robinson Crusoe,* and *Treasure Island.*

When Eve writes, she definitely sees pictures in her mind. "It's just like a movie strip unreeling," she says. "I sit and watch the movie and write it down. Sometimes the projector breaks down, and I have to yell out BOO! BOO! BOO!"

"In Ireland, it rained so much that I often sat and read. As a child, I read everything!"

If she gets stuck, she sometimes takes a hot bath. "I like to think in the bath," says Eve. "There, I'm closed away from everything. There is nothing to do but relax and think." She may also take a walk to think through a plot problem, which works "as long as I'm not walking with a friend, where we gabble."

Another cure for writer's block is to put the story aside for a while. "If I've written myself into a corner, or have lost sight of where I'm going, it sometimes works like magic if I leave the story alone for a while and do something else. If I get stuck while I'm working on a novel, I may have a picture book in mind, too, so I'll stop working on the novel and concentrate on the picture book. I'll let the novel go completely and then go back and start up again." Often, she'll find that the problem has worked itself out. "The solutions can be magic. They just come."

Eve finds ideas everywhere and anywhere. Some of them come from reading the newspaper. "I sometimes get ideas for young-adult books from something heartrending or bizarre that

I read in the newspaper," she says. One of her books, *Such Nice Kids,* was inspired by a newspaper article. In that book, a group of boys from a good school have an evening out, borrowing one of their mother's cars without her permission. They get into an accident and need money to fix the car. One of the boys has a gun. They decide to rob a convenience store. One thing leads to another, as they go from crime to crime. One of the boys gets killed.

By Eve Bunting · Illustrated by Ronald Himler

"I think it's good to write a story with a little something hidden, a message, something to make the reader think, 'Well, that was a wrong step,'" says Eve. "The reader can see how much better it would have been for my characters if they had just owned up right at the beginning."

Eve has advice for kids who like to write: "Read, read, read, and keep a journal. Not a journal that's for the classroom, but a journal that's for you to put everything in, your emotions, what you're thinking. I think that will help you."

What would Eve say to a kid who wanted to write but had been discouraged by a teacher, as she once was? "I would say, what a writer really needs is persistence and faith in herself. That's one of the hardest things to do, to have faith and persistence in the face of rejection and discouragement. But it must be cultivated. You have to write your way up and through. It's not easy."

The value of persistence and faith is evident. Just look at the shelves bulging with books written by Eve Bunting and enjoyed by so many readers.

DO IT YOURSELF!

Try Eve Bunting's idea. Scour the newspaper until you find a really interesting article. Then use it as a springboard for creating a suspenseful tale. Feel free to change the details to make your story stronger.

Bruce Coville

BORN: May 16, 1950, in Syracuse, New York
HOME: Syracuse, New York

SELECTED TITLES

Bruce Coville acknowledges that the original concept for his well-known book, *My Teacher Is an Alien*, wasn't his. "The name of the book and the concept were thought up by Byron Preiss," says Bruce. A writer, editor and book packager, Byron Preiss often sells ideas to publishing companies and then finds writers to write books based on his ideas.

"I wish I *had* thought of it," says Bruce. "It's the best title I've ever heard in my life." Byron's instincts and Bruce's writing talent were a potent combination. The book has sold well over a million copies.

Outlines are an integral part of Bruce's writing process. "When I was young and hungry, I thought it would be boring to write from an outline," he says. "What I found out was that the outline serves as a skeleton or frame for the book. Even writing from an outline, there are always surprises along the way. I always get where I mean to go but never by the route I expected to take."

LOTS OF REVISION

Bruce tends to rewrite a lot: between 4 and 13 rewrites is common, he says. For *Sarah's Unicorn*, one of his first books, Bruce says, "I did 40 or 50 rewrites." He now jokingly describes that behavior as obsessive-compulsive. Bruce was teaching school at the time and he says, "Every morning I would wake up, rewrite *Sarah's Unicorn*, go teach school, come home, go to sleep, wake up, and rewrite *Sarah's Unicorn*.

I spent six months on those five pages."

He often writes in the middle of the night, which is a holdover from the years when, he says, he held a day job to support his writing habit. "I used to think I couldn't wait until I could afford to write in the daytime and stop all the other nonsense," says Bruce. "No other jobs. Have a schedule like a human being. But then I found out that I write better in the middle of the night. So I started to make myself get up in the middle of the night."

If Bruce gets stuck, he likes to go for a walk. "That can be a problem in Syracuse, New York, on January 13 at 3:00 A.M. when it's 10 degrees below zero. But it's sometimes the best way for me to break through a plot point." He thinks he gets some of his best ideas while he's driving or taking a shower. "I engage the top part of my brain, so the creative underbrain can get its messages out," he says.

As a child, Bruce liked reading

Nancy Drew and *Hardy Boys* books. He also enjoyed *Dr. Doolittle, Mary Poppins*, and horse books written by Marguerite Henry and Walter Farley. He first discovered he liked writing when he was in sixth grade. "I had Miss Crandall for a teacher. All year long, she kept giving us specific assignments. I failed at those. Then she told me to write a short story. That was glorious. I found something that I really loved to do."

"My advice to kids is: Save all the stories you write and keep a good journal."

Bruce never intended to write funny books. "I thought I was going to write adventure stories," he says. "I wanted to be Edgar Rice Burroughs when I grew up. [Burroughs wrote numerous books, including the *Tarzan* series]. But I guess I have a loose wire in my head, because when I start out to write adventures, funny things happen."

To those who like to write, Bruce advises: "Write. Read. Keep a journal and *keep* the journal. Don't let anything happen to it. In 20 years it will become an absolute gold mine. It's hard to imagine you'll forget things, but can you remember the first day of first grade? It's all packed away in your underbrain. You need a mental fishing rod to get it out. Save a life. Write a journal. Things fade away. Keep contact with your past. I would love to have a journal of my fifth- or sixth-grade years, to know what I was really thinking. Save the stories you write, too."

Bruce hopes that kids will realize how much power they can have in their lives if they get a good education. He says: "You are born naked, ugly,

and helpless. Your whole job is to get powerful. By the time you come out of school, you should be able to use written and spoken language well, to gain power over your world. You can get attention by screaming, but you can't really make any changes. You make changes by using powerful arguments, tools of rhetoric, fine speaking, good rhythm."

He believes that storytelling ability is what separates human beings from other animals. "A couple of years ago, I wrote a book about prehistoric people. I wondered what made a human being. What separates us from animals? When did we cross the line?" He thought about this question for a long time. "Is it because we make tools? Chimpanzees make tools, too. Is it because human beings use language? Other animals do, too. What finally separates us?" Bruce thinks he has the answer. "We're the only species that can take ideas out of our heads, put them on paper, and share them with ourselves, with the person sitting across the desk from us, or across the room, or the person who will live in a hundred years. That's what we do that no other species does. That's what defines us as human beings."

Susan and Peter's sixth grade class has been invaded....

MY TEACHER IS AN ALIEN

by Bruce Coville

A MINSTREL BOOK

DO IT YOURSELF!

Here is a writing activity from Bruce Coville: "Take the first sentence from a book. Then try to write the opposite of the sentence by choosing the opposite for each word. The sentence may start, "The dark house on the crooked street...." What is the opposite of dark? Dark is a word with lots of shades of meaning. What you choose as the word's opposite tells a lot about you. When you're done, you'll have a well-constructed sentence that is entirely different from the one that you started with. And it just may help you get started on a story."

AUTHOR

Cynthia DeFelice

BORN: December 28, 1951, in Philadelphia, Pennsylvania
HOME: Geneva, New York

SELECTED TITLES

The Strange Night Writing of Jessamine Colter
1988

The Dancing Skeleton
1989

Weasel
1990

Devil's Bridge
1992

When Grandpa Kissed His Elbow
1992

The Light of Hogback Hill
1993

◇

Cynthia DeFelice wants to write books where kids can lose themselves, go on adventures, can live other lives. "I want them to want to keep turning the pages and be absorbed in that reality for a while, and when they finish reading the book and they close it and set it aside, they don't want it to end. I hope I've created characters and thoughts and ideas that they're going to come back to after they finish reading the book." Cynthia says she can't imagine a better reaction to one of her books than when a reader says, "I felt as if I was in that book."

Cynthia was one of four children. Her father worked several nights a week. "On those nights, we'd sit in a big chair in my parents' bedroom and Mom would read with enthusiasm, loving what she was doing just as much as we did. I remember that so fondly. All those stories became part of me."

After working in a bookstore, as a barn painter, and at the local newspaper, Cynthia became a children's librarian. Along the way, she found that she enjoyed telling stories, as well as reading them aloud. She teamed up with the school music teacher, Mary DeMarsh. They called themselves The Wild Washerwomen, and started by performing at school assemblies. Word of their talent soon spread, and Cynthia began to get lots of phone calls. "I hear you're a storyteller," the callers would say.

"I am?" Cynthia would respond, and then, collecting herself, she'd answer, "Well, sure." Before long,

Cynthia had enough work as a storyteller to quit her job as a librarian. She also had what she calls an "itch in her brain" that she wanted to scratch. She wanted to try writing a book. She gave herself one year. "I figured, if it doesn't work out, I can get another job as a librarian." During that year, she wrote *The Strange Night Writing of Jessamine Colter*, and was lucky enough to have it accepted for publication. Even though she had loved her work as a librarian, she never went back.

A WRITER AND STORYTELLER

Combining work as a writer and a storyteller has been productive. "The storytelling nurtures the writing, and vice versa," says Cynthia. "It's also a fun way for me to stay in touch with the kids I'm writing for." As a storyteller, Cynthia relishes the instant feedback she gets from her audience. "When I'm in front of a group of kids telling a story, I can see their faces. I know what's working. This lets me try out ideas."

When Cynthia wrote *Weasel*, she began with the idea of two kids alone in a cabin. "I started to ask myself questions. Where are the parents? What happened to the mother and father? Who is this guy at the door? Why doesn't he talk? Then I got to a certain point where I had to place the story in time." Cynthia was interested in the Removal Act, which was instituted in the 1830s to resettle Native Americans from their homelands to new reservations. She decided to set the story in a wilderness area where this resettlement had taken place. "I began to do in-depth research to place the book in a particular setting."

> ## "I want to create the experience that I had when I was a kid reading books. I just jumped into the story."

The process was different for her newest book of historical fiction, *Lost Man's River*. This story began with the setting—Ten Thousand Islands in Florida, about 1905. Says Cynthia, "The area is a maze of wild mangrove keys near the Everglades. It's very easy to get lost there." Cynthia had been to the area and had read some of its history. "The only people in this godforsaken place were remnants of the Seminole nation," says Cynthia. They had been chased there from the Carolinas and Georgia. The U.S. Army fought three wars against them in Florida. Eventually, about 500 Seminoles slipped off into the swamps. "The U.S. Army couldn't follow them. The islands had other people living on them too—plume hunters, who were wiping out the egret population [their plumes were worth their weight in gold], gator

skinners, crocodile and alligator poachers, and moonshiners. Anyone else down there was a runaway hiding for some reason."

Lost Man's River is about a family hiding out in the Ten Thousand Islands. The main character is a 13-year-old boy whose father was accused of murder in New York. "For every sentence I wrote, I had to do research," she says. "I had to be able to picture the scenes in my mind and be there myself."

Cynthia advises would-be writers to read a lot. "I really think it helps. I don't know any writer who isn't a reader. The idea isn't that you will copy things that you have read, but that all the wonderfully written sentences and plots you have read will be inside of you. You'll know how to write a good story, because you'll have read so many of them.

"Have experiences, meet people, keep your eyes and ears open. Notice things, such as how people talk, so that you can use these things in your writing. I don't think that writers are necessarily more sensitive or observant than anybody else. The only difference is, when something happens, they say to themselves, 'I'm going to write about this someday,' and they do."

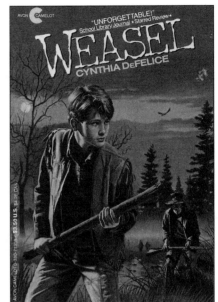

DO IT YOURSELF!

Here is a writing activity from Cynthia DeFelice: "*Casey and the Bath* and *Weasel* both start with a knock at the door. When a story begins this way, questions immediately come to mind. Who's in the house? Who's on the other side of the door? What are they doing there? What's going to happen next? It's such a simple, exciting way to start a story." Try it!

Sid Fleischman

BORN: March 16, 1920, in Brooklyn, New York
HOME: Santa Monica, California

Sid Fleischman began his career on the stage, in the waning days of vaudeville, as a magician. His specialty was sleight-of-hand. Sid started learning about magic when he was in the fifth grade. "That really was kind of the gyro of my early school years," he remembers. "I didn't read very much, at least not what other kids were reading. I read magic books." The first book he wrote, published when he was a teenager, was about magic. Since then, he has written five books about magic, as well as more than 35 children's books, 10 adult novels, and numerous screenplays.

Every time Sid gets ready to begin a new book, he sets up what he calls a "research book." He points out that he doesn't use 3-by-5-inch cards. "They drive me crazy. I can never find the darned things or keep them in order." If he were going to start a new book tomorrow, he'd get a blank book with a lot of tabs to break it into categories. "If the subject was the Civil War," he explains, "I'd have categories for articles of clothing, prices of things, flora and fauna, plot ideas, scene ideas, and character ideas."

He writes down everything that he finds out about the topic, "making room for the story ideas as I go along." Sid admits that most of the material is never used, at least not right away. "But it might turn up three or four books later." He always keeps that notebook with him when he's working on a book.

Sid uses a computer for writing,

commenting, "I have accepted the 20th century." He points out, though, that his son Paul (who won the Newbery Medal for his book of poems *Joyful Noise*) does not. "He still writes with a pencil," says Sid.

AN UNUSUAL METHOD

Sid's method of writing is, by his own description, eccentric. "I don't write a rough draft," he explains. "Most authors do. They'll suffer through the thing, just to get it down on paper. I don't work that way at all. I work on one page over and over again. Then I go to page 2. When I get to page 150, the book is ready for the printer. If I'm still on page 1 five months later, I know I've made a mistake. But when I find where I'm going, it's satisfying."

Unfortunately, in Sid's opinion, "Writing one book doesn't teach you how to write the next one." When he was a beginner and "not too confident," he used to outline extensively. Now he doesn't plan a book in advance. "When I start, I really don't know where it's going to end."

Sid writes in a "much-too-big" room on the lower floor of his two-story home. He begins working 15 minutes after he gets up in the morning. There is an orange tree in his backyard. On his way to his desk, he stops there to pick an orange, if there is one, and squeezes it for juice. He takes the glass of juice to his desk and starts writing. "I take a break, maybe a shower, after a couple of hours." Halfway through the day, he takes a nap. Then he works in the afternoon for a couple of hours, and sometimes at night as well. "When I'm done with a book, I'm apt to hop a freighter and go to Europe for a month."

> **"My magician's mind is very much at work when I'm writing stories. Like a magician, I can use magic to see around corners."**

Sid writes both books and film scripts. He says it's refreshing to write film scripts because no descriptive writing is necessary. "In a novel, if I have a couple of characters walk into a restaurant, I have to describe everything in the scene. In a script, everything but the dialogue and some bare-bones description is someone else's job." On the other hand, he says, a novel is published more or less as it is written, whereas with a script, it's after it's written that the trouble starts. "Everyone on the project becomes a literary expert." It is not uncommon for a script to go through numerous rewrites.

He is an extremely visual writer. "I see things projected. I just have that kind of mind." When he gets stuck, which sometimes happens, he accepts the situation as "just part of the game.

Mostly I stick with it, but if I can't, I go away and come back. You can't expect things to go swimmingly day in and day out. Besides, you develop more of an affection for the books that give you trouble than the ones that come easily."

Sid doesn't speak to school groups anymore, but when he did, he always tried to encourage the students in his audience who wanted to be writers. "You never know who is sitting out there," he says. "It could be another William Saroyan." He also suggests that would-be writers remember that writing has to be practiced. "A violinist knows he can't just pick up a violin and play at Carnegie Hall," says Sid. "Most kids don't realize that writing needs the same sort of discipline and practice." He tells kids to build their vocabularies and their understanding of what other authors have done.

When not writing or traveling, Sid likes to garden. "I grow corn in my front yard," he says. He also spends time in his greenhouse, which he built to grow watermelons and honeydew. He loves growing things, although he admits, with a laugh, "I figured out once that it costs me about $25 to grow each honeydew. And the ones in the store taste better." He also likes astronomy and classical guitar, though he "spent five years trying to learn to play one piece."

Sid is encouraged when he gets letters from kids that say "I don't like to read, but I've read one of your books 16 times." He says, "It makes me feel that all the agonies I've been through were worth it."

SID FLEISCHMAN
The Whipping Boy

illustrations by PETER SIS

DO IT YOURSELF!

Here is a writing activity from Sid Fleischman: "Write a story based on this premise—Your parents call you into the living room. 'I have something to tell you,' says your mother. 'Your father is actually from outer space.'"

Russell Freedman

BORN: October 11, 1929, in San Francisco, California
HOME: New York, New York

Russell Freedman has written more than 30 books for children. Many of those books are biographies of famous people, including Abraham Lincoln, Eleanor Roosevelt, and a forthcoming book about photographer Louis Hine. In Russell's opinion, biographies written for children have changed dramatically in recent years.

In the past, that type of book relied heavily on imaginary scenes and invented dialogue, with the writer making up conversations that might have taken place in a character's life. It was through invented dialogue that the 200-year-old myth of George Washington's confession about chopping down his father's cherry tree was born. "Nobody writes invented dialogue anymore," says Russell. "It isn't necessary. There's such a wealth of documentary material to draw from—journals, letters, diaries, and autobiographies. Quoting from these sources takes the place of invented dialogue."

When Russell prepares to write a biography, he begins by "soaking" himself in his subject. "I start reading about it and thinking about it and I absorb the subject to as great an extent as possible. I start planning the book in my head." For a recent biography of Eleanor Roosevelt, Russell read 30 or 40 books about her life. He knows he is ready to begin writing when he feels as though he has gotten to know his character very well—so well that he can tell himself stories about the character without looking them up.

Russell writes on what he calls a Humphrey Bogart typewriter. He says one reason he doesn't want to use a computer is superstition. "This typewriter has been extraordinarily lucky for me. I like to type every draft. The first draft is usually a mess. I would never allow anybody to see it. It's a jumble. Simply trying to get all this raw material down on paper is the most painful part of the writing process for me. Once I can start revising the first draft, I begin to have fun. At that point I will refer back to my notes to make sure that I am getting it right."

FINDING THE RHYTHM
Each manuscript goes through four or five drafts. "I type every draft from beginning to end. If I start at the first word and have to type the whole thing, I have the rhythm of the prose. I catch things that are missing. I see things that are in there that shouldn't be."

The room where Russell writes is large, with windows on two sides, a lot of bookshelves, an old beat-up desk with a modern desk chair, and his old typewriter. Over his desk dangles a model of a Wright Brothers airplane that he bought in Paris. "It's a beautiful wooden handmade airplane, a toy, that hangs like a mobile from the ceiling. It has a battery in it. You press the button and a propeller goes around. It flies in a circle right over my desk. I turn it on once in a while when I want to cheer myself up."

"If you gave a kid today one of the biographies I read in grade school, you'd be laughed right out of the room."

◇

Though Russell has written nonfiction books on a wide variety of topics, these days he mostly writes biographies. "Writing a biography is like getting to know a person," he says. "You get to know that person better than you know yourself. You study them with such intensity. You read everything there is to read about them and anything they ever said about themselves. You go to bed thinking about that person. You wake up thinking about that person."

Russell is glad he's chosen to write his biographies for children because he thinks writing adult-length biographies would not suit his temperament. "An adult biography takes five years or longer to write," he says. "By doing what I do, I can write a different book every year."

To Russell, writing nonfiction books for children is an art form because "they have to have their own power and pace to carry the reader along. You have to include everything that is important and leave out everything that isn't. In some ways, it is like poetry. It fits a certain form and restricts itself. Yet I believe you can say a great deal in a children's biography."

When asked if he has pictures in his mind when he writes, Russell replies, "Of course. That's what writing is." He adds that in the case of historical nonfiction, the mental pictures he has must be the product of meticulous research. "I don't attempt to describe a room unless I have evidence of what it looked like."

For example, Russell's book on Eleanor Roosevelt begins with what he feels is an important incident that showed something about the relationship between Eleanor and her mother and about Eleanor's self-image as a young girl. The scene opens with Eleanor standing at the doorway of a room in her childhood home. "I had enough evidence from what I had read to describe every piece of furniture in that room. I even knew what the silver tea set that sat on the table beside her mother looked like. Otherwise, I wouldn't have attempted to do it."

Russell has always liked to write. He wrote a comic strip in grade school, and he had pieces in every school publication. He wrote fiction and poetry in high school and college. After college, he became a journalist. Through it all Russell says, "I've always thought of myself as somebody who was a writer."

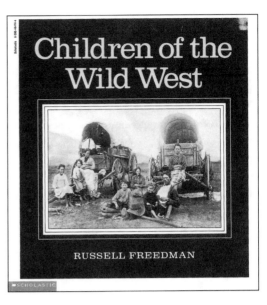

DO IT YOURSELF!

Interview somebody you know, such as a grandparent, and write a brief biography with Russell Freedman looking over your shoulder. Be accurate and keep it interesting. Make sure you're true to the spirit of the person you're writing about.

Jean Craighead George

BORN: July 2, 1919, in Washington, D.C.
HOME: Chappaqua, New York

SELECTED TITLES

My Side of the Mountain
(Newbery Honor Book)
1959

The Summer of the Falcon
1962

Julie of the Wolves
(Newbery Medal)
1972

The Wounded Wolf
1978

The Talking Earth
1983

One Day in the Prairie
1986

Water Sky
1987

Shark Beneath the Reef
1989

On the Far Side of the Mountain
1990

The First Thanksgiving
1993

—◇—

Jean Craighead George spent her childhood summers at an old family home in Pennsylvania, where her father grew up. "There were fish in the creek, and big, open meadows," remembers Jean. "Kids today just don't have the freedom, which is so creative, to wander all by themselves beside a creek in a meadow of flowers. That is just the perfect thing for the mind. I still do that as often as possible. I hike and walk a lot."

It was Jean's love of nature and the animal world that first brought her to Alaska, where she found the inspiration for her Newbery award-winning book, *Julie of the Wolves*. She had read of some scientific investigations about wolf behavior, and she wanted to write an article about wolf research. Jean and her son Luke traveled to Barrow, Alaska, in 1970 to find out more about the topic. In her acceptance speech for the Newbery Medal, Jean described an important incident that took place just after their arrival at the small wooden air terminal on the tundra in Barrow: "As we waited for our luggage, Luke pointed to a small fur-clad child who was walking into the wilderness over which we had just flown. 'She's awfully little to be going that way alone,' he said, shoving his hands deep into his pockets and stepping closer to me. The little girl walked with determination, her straight back expressing confidence and inner strength. Months later, she, of course, was to become Julie."

On that same journey to Alaska, Jean and Luke were able to spend 10 days out on the tundra, observing the behavior of a pack of wolves. "I've been out howling with the wolves," she declares proudly. It is that type of direct experience, combined with her elegant sense of story, that makes her writing so dramatic and so unforgettable.

A LIFE IN NATURE

The natural world has been important to Jean all her life and has profoundly influenced her work. "We took our children out into nature from the time they were very young. We caught frogs and taught them about plants and animals." To Jean, teaching children about nature is like teaching them about religion: "If you catch them young enough, you've got them."

Another son, Craig, now lives in Barrow, Alaska. Says Jean, "He has been hired by Eskimos to study bowhead whale populations. When the International Whaling Commission said there should be no more hunting of bowheads, the Eskimos responded, 'Whales are the basis of our culture. We must hunt them in moderation. There are a lot more out there than you think.'" They hired naturalists like Craig to count the whales as they passed by in migration. The whale-counters have confirmed that the bowhead population is at least 14,000, almost the number there was in the days before Yankee whaling. Craig's work with whales served as an inspiration for Jean's book *Water Sky*, which is about native hunting of bowheads in Alaska.

"When you're polishing and fitting the right words in the right places, writing becomes thrilling."

Jean carries little spiral notebooks with her on her forays into the natural world. "I take notes all the time," she says. She also has a laptop computer, but she's decided not to use it anymore. "If I'm carrying it while I'm hiking around, and I want to stop and write something down, I have to open it up, sit down, and start it. It's easier for me to just use my own pencil and paper." An accomplished artist who has illustrated many of her own books, Jean also sketches a lot as she hikes.

Reflecting on her sequel to *Julie of the Wolves*, Jean says, "I'm amazed that my publisher suggested that I do it. I didn't think I could." At first, she had no idea where to begin. "Then I realized I had set myself up in the first book to answer some interesting questions in a sequel. The wolves are a threat to Julie's father's musk oxen. He had to become a wolf hunter to protect the musk oxen in the village. But Julie disagrees. That's what the book is about."

Sometimes Jean will redo a book from the beginning if she's dissatisfied with how it came out. "I put *My Side of the Mountain* on the shelf and started it over again." That's not as daunting as it might seem, Jean says, because "I had the whole story in my head." She calls her first drafts "first runs." "My first run is to get to know all the people and see how they're moving. I let the movie run in my head. But there are times when things get out of focus!" Jean likes this way of writing because "when you really know the story and all the people, you can write so much more clearly. I find that there are a lot of sentences I have in my early drafts that I really don't need."

Most children's books tell a story in order, because many children's writers and editors believe children don't like flashbacks. Jean doesn't agree. She began *Julie of the Wolves* in the middle and then went back to explain why her main character was living with a pack of wolves. "Children are my audience," she explains. "I want to grab them on the first page, if possible, and keep them to the last page."

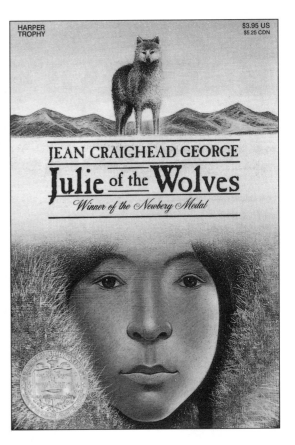

HARPER TROPHY $3.95 US $5.25 CDN

JEAN CRAIGHEAD GEORGE
Julie of the Wolves
Winner of the Newbery Medal

DO IT YOURSELF!

Here is a writing activity from Jean Craighead George: "Right now, I'm looking out my window at a green forsythia stalk against a brilliant red bush. All kinds of things are happening to that twig. Bugs are crawling up it. Birds are flying past it. I begin to write...." Now it's your turn. Open your eyes and jot down what *you* see. Even if you're just looking down at your sneakers, there's a story waiting to be written.

Bette Greene

BORNE: June 28, 1934, in Parkin, Arkansas
HOME: Brookline, Massachusetts

SELECTED TITLES

Summer of My German Soldier
1973

Philip Hall Likes Me, I Reckon Maybe
(Newbery Honor Book)
1974

Get on Out of Here, Philip Hall
1981

Them That Glitter and Them That Don't
1983

Morning Is a Long Time Coming
1988

The Drowning of Stephan Jones
1991

◇

To be a writer, Bette Greene believes, requires three basic abilities: "being able to use words with consummate skill; having a kamikaze's approach to living; and having the ability to look at yourself without seeing yourself as either a hero or a clown. That is hard, because none of us is as beautiful as we would like to believe we are." There is another quality that Bette believes is essential to becoming a writer, too "You have to be driven."

A student once came up to Bette and said, "I can't decide whether to be a writer or a computer programmer." Bette replied that there was no doubt about it, that the girl should be a computer programmer. The author remembers, "She looked at me as though I were a genius and asked me how I knew that. I replied, 'The world isn't waiting for another novelist, though there are always new ones trying to crawl their way up.'" Bette says that writers really have to believe in what they're doing, or nothing will happen.

Believing in herself and in her work helped Bette when she was trying to get her favorite of her own works published. *Summer of My German Soldier* was turned down by 17 publishers before it was finally accepted. "They said there was no market for it because it was a story told by a 12-year old," says Bette. "Editors thought that a book told by a 12-year-old would only be read by children 11 and younger. No one wants to read a book narrated by someone who is younger than they are. And the publishers thought the ideas presented in the book were too mature for an 11-year-old to comprehend."

But Bette persisted in submitting the manuscript because she believed in it. And today, she has the satisfaction of saying that the book has gone through more than 30 printings in 20 years—proof of its long-term popularity and influence.

THE MAGIC IN THE PAPER

When Bette gets ready to write a book, she thinks about it and waits until a story haunts her. She writes with a fountain pen, filled with ink from an ink bottle, on yellow or white legal pads. "If I'm not writing well with one pen, I put it away," she says. "Sometimes I'll change the paper, too. We're always looking for the magic that's in the paper. Intellectually I know that the magic is neither in the pen nor in the paper. It's a little bit like the Japanese tea ceremony. You tell yourself, 'This paper is going to do it for me. This is where I'm going to get the gift of the story.'"

After writing with a pen for a time, Bette turns to her computer to do rewrites. "I use the pen first, rather than anything mechanical, because the pen is more of an extension of me. It's more natural." She recommends to her students that they use a pen rather than a pencil because "a fountain pen has more drama. It's more definitive. There's nothing wishy-washy about it. You have to suffer when you use a pen, for you end up with permanently stained fingers."

"I had what I think was the best training in the world for a writer: I grew up in a place where I was different."

As a child growing up in Arkansas, Bette thought she was the best writer in her class. But, she says, "I never received more than a C or a C- in composition. I had trouble with spelling and punctuation and neatness." But she didn't let her average grades discourage her. "Young people have to be their own cheering squad," she believes. "If you're your own cheering squad, down the road, the world will pick up on it. Then you can say, 'What's the fuss? I knew I was great when I was nine years old!'"

When Bette grew up, she moved to New York City for a while, where she went to a lot of plays. "I discovered what all those critics had always talked about: The performing arts are much more advanced than the creative arts. So if you were an actor, you were at a much higher level in your art than playwrights, poets, or novelists."

Bette decided to take acting

lessons. She reasoned that by studying acting, she might be able to figure out what made actors special as creative artists, and to see if she could transpose this extra measure of creativity to her work as a writer. "I studied acting with a woman who was a proponent of the Stanislavski Method." (Konstantin Stanislavski, the director of the Moscow Art Theatre in the early 20th century, devised an acting technique known popularly as the "Method." Method acting involves drawing upon personal experiences to bring out the emotions of the characters portrayed.)

Bette believes that the Method has made her a more insightful writer. This exercise, which she has tried, illustrates her point: "What does it feel like to be thirsty? You think you know, but you don't. If I were writing a scene where my characters were thirsty in the desert, I would go without water for a day. Then I would take careful notes about what it feels like to be without water." She tries to teach this approach to her many writing students, as well.

DO IT YOURSELF!

Here is a writing activity from Bette Greene: Write a scene in which your main character is getting in deeper and deeper trouble. Write it in the form of a narrative, a play, or a poem. If you're feeling ambitious, write another scene—one that gets the character *out* of the trouble.

Johanna Hurwitz

BORN: October 9, 1937, in New York, New York
HOME: Great Neck, New York

SELECTED TITLES

Busybody Nora
1976

The Law of Gravity
1978

Aldo Applesauce
1979

Baseball Fever
1981

The Rabbi's Girls
1982

Tough-Luck Karen
1982

The Adventures of Ali Baba Bernstein
1985

The Hot and Cold Summer
1985

Class Clown
1987

Russell Sprouts
1987

Hurray for Ali Baba Bernstein
1989

Roz and Ozzie
1992

◇

Once, when Johanna Hurwitz was speaking to a group of kids, one of them asked her if all of the characters from all of her books would ever meet each other. "I liked that question," she remembers. "I've been trying to work it out ever since." She thinks it may happen someday. "You know how I think I'd do it? I'd have all of them go on a vacation someplace (since they all live in different parts of the country), and they'd all stay in the same motel."

In her books, Johanna has often included characters with personalities like people she has known. The characters of Nora and her brother Teddy, who are in Johanna's series of Nora books, are based on Johanna's children. "They live in an apartment building in New York City, just like we did." She even sees herself in some of her writing. "Sometimes I can point a finger at a character or an action or a reaction and know it was something I did." But she didn't model the mother in the Nora series on herself. "That mother is much more patient and much better than I was. One of the wonderful things about being a writer is that you can use things from your own life, but you can make your characters so that they react to situations perfectly."

ALWAYS A READER

Books have always been very important to Johanna, so important that when she was younger she didn't always understand that they might not be as important to other people. "I

remember once as a child talking with a friend about a book that I'd read. That girl wasn't a reader. I said, 'When you read, don't you see it like a movie?' She didn't. She was trying to read a book I had read and liked. I realized that a non-reader can't make the transition from words to pictures in her head."

When Johanna grew up and became a librarian, she always tried to help kids find "breakthrough books" that they could relate to like movies. Johanna believes that every reader has a breakthrough book. There was a little girl who came every day to the library where Johanna used to work. She would check out an armload of books and bring them back the next day. "She never read them," remembers Johanna. "I don't know what her home life was like, but she liked the library. Every day, she wanted to know about the books I handed to her. I'd give her one of my little book talks. She'd come back the next day. One day, she came back with

Stuart Little and said, 'Do you think he's going to find the bird?' I don't know if it was something I said, or if it was the pictures in the book. After that, she didn't take out so many books." Johanna knew that another reader had been born.

Before she writes a book, Johanna thinks about it a lot. "I take notes all the time," she says. "I have a drawer full of little papers with notes." When she sees something that might pertain to one of her books, she makes a note of it. When she's writing, she puts all the notes together.

"When I was growing up, everybody important in books seemed to be named Betsy."

Johanna thinks she's a little different from many other writers in this way: "I don't work with an outline. I know where I'm beginning and where I want to end. I don't always know the middle." She compares this to taking a trip and leaving the map at home. "If you're going to Washington, D.C. from New York City, you want to go south. You might get on the highway, you might take a detour that takes longer, you might get lost, you might waste some time. You might also end up somewhere you didn't expect to be! You might have some adventure you didn't expect to have, or find some surprises along the way."

Johanna cheerfully admits that when she writes, she wastes time. "I go into dead ends. I throw away whole chunks of writing that are irrelevant to what I was writing about." But those detours are sometimes valuable. "Some of the best things I've written have been surprises that came up when the writing took a little detour

as it went along the way."

Why does she write this way? Says Johanna, "If I sat down to read a book and knew everything that was going to happen, I'd be bored. For me, it's the same thing with writing." Sometimes, one of her characters says something she didn't expect the character to say. Then Johanna says to the character, "I didn't know you were going to say that!"

To begin each writing session, Johanna writes a warm-up letter to a friend. "It gets me started thinking, and it keeps me up-to-date with my correspondence." She has one friend to whom she's written warm-up letters two or three times a week for years.

Johanna likes the life of a writer, though it's different from what she thought it would be. "When I was growing up, I assumed you couldn't write until you'd gone out and lived some very exciting life," she explains. "I'm still waiting for that to happen to me. I've discovered that everybody's life has little interesting things happening. But you just have to realize that what goes on in your life is interesting, and that what happens in books can be based on ordinary lives, too."

DO IT YOURSELF!

Here is a writing activity from Johanna Hurwitz: "One of my characters is a boy named David Bernstein, who picks a new first name for himself. I sometimes ask kids if they know where their own names came from. If they don't, I suggest that they go home and find out." If you could pick any other name, which one would you pick? How would it make you feel to have that name? Write about it.

Mavis Jukes

BORN: May 3, 1947, in Nyack, New York
HOME: Cotati, California

Mavis Jukes takes lots of notes when she's writing books. "Actually," she says, "I take notes and lose them. I scribble on the backs of envelopes and important receipts in the pickup truck that end up getting thrown behind the seat and lost. Then I drive myself crazy lying in bed at night. I worry that I have lost this great idea that I was going to put into the book." But, she finds, "lost ideas often come back around."

Mavis's manuscripts always seem to sit around for a while before they are finished. Not because she wants them to, but because she's busy working with her editor to make them good books. Besides, Mavis's days are busy. "I'm a wife and a mother of two adolescent girls, and I have three dogs and a sheep and a cat. Because of my lifestyle, everything has to sit around for a few hours or weeks before I can get back to it."

This doesn't bother her. "I've discovered over the last few years that no time is lost. Ideas leak in, no matter what you're doing—like ideas that spring from conversations that you have with your kids on the way to the pediatrician's office."

RECOGNIZING THE ARTIST INSIDE

Mavis didn't set out to be a writer. First, she taught school for five years. "During that eye-opening period of my life, my students taught me a lot of stuff that I didn't know about," she says. Then she wanted to move into a position where she could help make some changes in society. So she decided to go to law school.

Mavis loved law school. "It was really interesting. I met a neat group of people. I was fascinated by the material." But when it came right down to it, she decided not to practice law. "I guess some kind of alarm went off inside me that said 'It's now or never. If you're going to do anything about recognizing the artist in you, you'd better hurry up.'"

She decided to become a writer because she felt that through writing she might also be able to initiate change in society. "Ultimately, I feel I do have more power as a writer than I would have had as a lawyer. I'm most interested in addressing young people, and this way I can."

When Mavis was a kid, she didn't have much time for reading. "I liked the idea of reading and felt I should be reading," she remembers. "I would make a big order of paperback books from the book clubs at school. I'd fill out the order forms and forget to bring in my money. My mother would come in with a check, and then I'd come home with a big stack of books, but I never read them."

Instead, Mavis did other things. She grew up on a little farm on the east coast. "Looking back, I had a very active fantasy life going on," she says. "I was really into playing cowboy. I had a long tenure as a sheriff. I also was a homemaker. I had an elaborate pretend house that was actually a yew bush with different rooms you could creep around in. I also had a communications system made out of orange-juice cans and wax string. We'd get into different trees and yell into the cans and think it was as good as a telephone."

"When you're a writer, you're continuously writing in your head."

The farm was full of animals— chickens, cats that were always having kittens ("which we would dress up"), a pet skunk, and a weasel. It was also always full of children. "We had a lot of kids over all the time," says Mavis. "My sister and I were always writing plays that starred ourselves." They had a lot of parties. "There were endless shenanigans."

Her days were full and happy. "By the time I hit the sack at 9:30, I'd chased the last butterfly out of the yard. I'd caught the last firefly to try to make a lantern." She was bushed—too tired for books.

Though she didn't like to read as a child, Mavis certainly did like to write. "I wrote a story called 'The Personal Pig.' My dad was very pleased with it. He had it 'published.' He asked someone in his office to type it with a piece of carbon paper. He

sent a couple of copies to his friends." It meant a lot to Mavis that her father took the time to share her story with his friends.

Mavis sees herself as a very visual writer. In fact, she has collaborated on several screenplays. "When I write, I write through the eye of a camera," she says. "I almost never write from inside of the person." She likes to make her readers work a little bit, too. "I like to leave it up to the kids to come to conclusions and figure out stuff." For example, rather than writing that a character has started to cry, Mavis might say that the character touched the corner of her eye with her shirt-sleeves. Or she might write, "He heard her snort," and expect readers to figure out that a character is laughing.

To those who want to write, Mavis advises: "Consider writing to be like making art, like painting or sculpture. Remember that what you observe is just as important to becoming a writer as what you write down. Give particular attention to details." She always tells kids to write about things that make them feel frustrated or bad or sad. "When you feel confused, lost, alienated, alone, and you write about your feelings, your writing can be like a life raft that you can climb on. It will take you safely to shore."

I'll See You in My Dreams

DO IT YOURSELF!

Here is a writing activity from Mavis Jukes: "Try to notice some details about where you live. What kind of cereal boxes are on the counter? What fruit is in the bowl? What's on the walls? What do you see around you that catches your eye? Notice some things about your physical environment, such as a can of coffee, a black flashlight with a red switch, a Chicago Bulls jacket, or a wood stove with ashes in it. Notice objects that you like, that you think are beautiful in some way, like a blue tea pot with a chip on the spout. Write about those things."

Jane Langton

BORN: December 30, 1922, in Boston, Massachusetts
HOME: Lincoln, Massachusetts

When Jane Langton is going to write a book, whether it's a work of fiction for children or a mystery book for adults, she begins by doing an enormous amount of research. She sometimes wonders if she does too much. "It's just awful," she says. "It would be much better if I just sat down and wrote down 'Page One,' and didn't do all that book reading and research."

The Fragile Flag, the story of a girl who tries to walk from Boston to Washington, D.C. to attend an antinuclear rally, was one of the few books Jane feels she didn't research too much. Still, for that book she and her son Andy drove from Boston to New York City along Route 1, with Jane writing down everything she saw on the way. Jane also took a very short walk along the very busy Route 128 outside Boston, to see what it felt like. "I wrote that book very quickly," she says. "I'm sure it's better for it." Jane lists *The Fragile Flag* as among her most favorite.

Another book of Jane's that required very little research was *The Fledgling*, the story of a girl who yearns to fly. Her research for that book was simple. "I just dreamed about flying," she says. "That's thrilling. In those dreams, I'm not really flying, but more like bounding, sort of bouncing along, and saying to myself, 'Well of course I can do this.' You just run and jump and up you go, and then you come down very softly." Jane wishes she dreamed about flying more often. "Most of my dreams are

boring, about folding the laundry."

Jane writes in a study with lots of sunlight pouring in. "It's messy," she says. "It contains all the remains of my earlier books, notebooks piled up with drawings, all sitting there in cardboard boxes." On the wall are lots of little notes of things Jane doesn't want to forget. One is a quote: "St. Bernard covered his head crossing the Alps to avoid seeing the beauty of the earth." Some are letters from children who have enjoyed her books. "There's a letter that I found it in my mailbox from a little girl. It was written on a pink piece of paper with a feather attached. She put it in my mailbox, not daring to come in to speak to me."

PICTURES BECOME WORDS

Each day, Jane puts off writing "as long as possible, by reading the newspaper." Still, she tries to get to work at least by 8:00, or preferably by 7:00. "My brain works in the morning," Jane explains. "My I.Q. goes down as the day goes on."

As she writes, she sees pictures. "I

should think every writer has to imagine herself at the scene and imagine being in the skin of the person, seeing what they see," says Jane. "I'm fond of the passage in the *The Fledgling* where Georgie is looking out the window and wanting to fly up to the goose, and she sees pieces of happiness coming up from the street." Jane explains the pictures she saw in her mind as she wrote that sequence. "Picture yourself looking out the window and feeling happy. The whole landscape feels happy. Describe what it is like to fly on the back of a goose, to feel the silken feathers and the rush of air, and to smell the fox. You just have to plunge yourself into this experience of imagination."

> ## "The story springs out of the place it's set in. So I have to know the place, and I have to know all the details about it."

As a child, Jane loved to read. She can still remember the bookshelf in the public library in Wilmington, Delaware that held her favorite books, by the British author Arthur Ransome. "I adored those," says Jane. "They were very straightforward, down-to-earth books about kids."

These days, Jane still reads a lot. "I have a bunch of books that are my favorites. I read them over and over and over. Among them are the *Letters of Virginia Woolfe*, and the works of Anthony Trollope." She also likes to "read" books on tape while she's working in her garden or getting supper or taking a bath. "I get a lot more reading done that way than I would without them," she says. "They're right with me all the time." Listening to books, says Jane, is "like sitting on your father's knee and being read a story. Dickens on tape is wonderful. Those great, great long books are so pure. I can't get enough of them. Hearing them is like being washed in a verbal blessing."

Jane loves to travel, mostly to places where she hopes to set a book. "I want very much to write a mystery set in the University Museum at Oxford," says Jane. "It would be a wonderful 19th-century book full of interest in relation to John Ruskin and Thomas Henry Huxley and Lewis Carroll, of all people." She wants to be able to spend enough time there to be able to "soak up the place— bathe in it, so to speak." And then, after doing "too much" research, she would begin her slow, careful work that yields such unforgettable results.

DO IT YOURSELF!

Jane Langton suggests: "Go to a store. Make a long list of how it feels to be there, the smells, the sights, the sounds. Take from that list just one thing that best captures the store. Write a sentence describing that most important thing in which you distill the feeling of the place. Anybody reading your sentence should say, 'Yes, that is what it is like to go into that store.' For example, the place I remember always smelled of marshmallows."

Kathryn Lasky

BORN: June 24, 1944, in Indianapolis, Indiana
HOME: Cambridge, Massachusetts

SELECTED TITLES

Tall Ships
1978

Dollmaker: The Eyelight and the Shadow
1981

The Night Journey
1981

The Weaver's Gift
1981

Jem's Island
1982

Sugaring Time
(Newbery Honor Book)
1983

Home Free
1985

Puppeteer
1985

Pageant
1986

The Bone Wars
1988

Sea Swan
1988

Dinosaur Dig
1990

Think Like an Eagle: At Work With a Wildlife Photographer
1992

My Island Grandma
1993

When Kathryn Lasky prepares to write a book, whether fiction or nonfiction, she begins with a research phase. "I usually get interested in a topic because of some little snippet of information that I've stumbled across," she says. That will pique Kathryn's interest. "I say to myself, 'This might make a really neat book.'"

Then she starts researching. About her research, Kathryn has written, "For me in writing, I am searching for the story among the truths, the facts, the lies, and the realities."

The research phase usually lasts "for a long time." She often starts at one of the many libraries near where she lives. But usually most of her research is done in the field. "In my own experience in writing," Kathryn explains, "I have always tried hard to listen, smell, and touch the places that I write about—especially if I am lucky enough to be there."

CREATING CHARACTERS

For her book *The Weaver's Gift*, Kathryn could not forget "the smell of the lanolin vapors rising from the merino sheep's back under the heat lamp of the lambing pen in the barn that early March morning." For her book *Dollmaker: The Eyelight and the Shadow*, Kathryn carried away the memory of the dollmaker, Carolee Bowling, "trembling and pale, as she made the mold of her doll's clay head. If the original were damaged, she would have to scrap two months worth of painstaking work." Watching Carolee work and feeling her tension, Kathryn was able to create a characterization that added dimension and scope to the story she told.

Sometimes her life experiences stand in the way of her writing. Her book *Tall Ships* is about a 14-year-old boy who lived in the 19th century and yearned to go to sea. When Kathryn was writing that book, she spent a lot of time studying the archives at the Peabody Museum in Salem, Massachusetts. She had even crossed the Atlantic twice, in small sailboats, "hating almost every minute of it." But she was having trouble writing about her character's experience. "Then I read that Samuel Eliot Morison had said that history is one-tenth fact and nine-tenths imagination. So I started imagining. That meant forgetting who I was and the fact that while I was crossing the Atlantic ocean, I would rather have been in Bloomingdale's. I had to imagine what it would have been like to be 14 in the year 1856 in a one-street town in Maine."

Kathryn recently came back from Mexico. She and her husband, a photographer, are collaborating on a book about the Mexican festival called Day of the Dead, which takes place at the same time as Halloween. It is a very elaborate, colorful festival, during which, as Kathryn describes it, "these joyous, healthy people go to graveyards." While in Mexico, she and her husband spent three days following a Mexican family through the phases of the holiday. To research other books, she's gone on dinosaur digs in South Dakota (resulting in *Dinosaur Dig* and *The Bone Wars*), to London to map out a trail her characters might take from one place to another, and to St. Croix to see leatherback turtles nesting on beaches (for two of the books in the *Starbuck* series).

"I've always tried hard to listen, smell, and touch the places that I write about."

◇

When her research is complete, she writes a very detailed proposal, which she sends to a publisher. "My proposals, especially for picture books and nonfiction books, are sometimes almost as long as the books themselves," says Kathryn. She recently submitted a 24-page proposal for a 32-page book!

Because she puts so much effort into her proposals, writing the books themselves happens fairly quickly. "After I write the proposal, I write an outline," says Kathryn. The outlines are bare bones at first: beginning, middle, end. "I just write down one idea for each heading. It might be a little scrap of dialogue, or a place where the story is going to start, or

what the situation is." Then she goes back and develops the first part, asking herself, "What do I want to happen?"

When writing a book recently on censorship, Kathryn created eleven outlines. "I kept breaking it down," she explains. "I outlined the first few chapters. Then I kept outlining smaller and smaller pieces. My outlines would be quite unintelligible to anybody else but me."

Kathryn enjoys challenging herself by writing books on different topics. About this, she has said, "I can't stand doing the same thing twice. I don't want to change just for the sake of change. But the whole point of being an artist is to be able to get up every morning and reinvent the world. It's a question of challenge."

Portions of the above first appeared in "Reflections on Nonfiction" by Kathryn Lasky, (*Horn Book*, September/October 1985) and "Creativity in a Boom Industry" by Kathryn Lasky (*Horn Book*, November/December 1991). Reprinted with permission of the Horn Book, Inc.

DO IT YOURSELF!

Kathryn suggests that you write about a ridiculous or funny situation that happened to you. Here's one she plans to write about: "I take tap dancing lessons. I was practicing tap dancing with my friend. We're in a private class that's held over at her house. Her kids have a hamster. He has a clear plastic ball that he can roll in, all around the house. We were tapping away, and all of a sudden, this hamster rolled in. The ball stopped at my feet. I nearly died laughing!"

AUTHOR

Bette Bao Lord

BORN: November 3, 1938, in Shanghai, China
HOME: New York, New York

Author Bette Bao Lord did not start out to write *In the Year of the Boar and Jackie Robinson* for children at all. "I started to write my book as an adults' book," remembers Bette, "but the voice was wrong." For her, finding a voice with which she is comfortable is the first part of the writing process. "It's different for each project I'm involved in," she says. In the case of *Year of the Boar* Bette found the voice by going back in time. "The book was 50 or 60 percent based on the true facts of my Americanization," says Bette, who emigrated from China when she was nine years old. "The right voice for that book was an innocent voice that belonged to a child. It did not belong to me as an adult."

In fact, *In the Year of the Boar and Jackie Robinson* is the only children's book Bette has ever written. (She is the author of several other books and numerous magazine articles for adults.) She liked writing for children, and says *Year of the Boar* is one of her favorite books that she has written. "I particularly liked the children's book because it gave me a chance to be funny," she says. "None of my other books was able to give me that outlet." Bette thinks that the girl in the book is very like herself. "She's very foolish. She's very daring. I did actually get lost the first day I was in Brooklyn. That particular incident is true. I like to think about this child landing in a new country and expecting she could get around by herself."

Bette did not even originally intend to be a writer. "When my sister got out of China, after she and I had been separated for 17 years, I learned her story and wanted somebody to write it. I thought it was so moving and powerful, and nothing like it had been written." As a child, Bette had been very moved by *The Diary of Anne Frank*. She thought her sister's story was comparable in some ways because it, too, involved a painful childhood in a troubled time. Bette's sister spoke only Chinese. Bette couldn't find a writer who could speak Chinese, so she decided to write the book herself. Her sister's story became the book *Eighth Moon: The True Story of a Young Girl's Life in Communist China*.

THROUGH THE TUNNEL
To start writing, Bette has to feel herself completely alone. She describes approaching a writing project as being "like going down a very long, dark, scary tunnel." Each day she tries to write, she has to walk through that tunnel, in her own imagination. "I do not advise anybody

to follow my example," she laughs. "I have to spend a lot of time just sitting there getting into that book or that piece of writing. I have not been able to shorten the process." Bette compares herself to Alice in *Alice in Wonderland*, whose fantasy adventure began when she slipped down the rabbit hole. "Without going down the rabbit hole, I can't seem to function," she says.

Bette usually works late at night. "My prime time for working is between 10:00 and 3:00 or 4:00. The darkness is important, for some reason or other." On her desk sits a bust of Abraham Lincoln. "As you can tell, I hope, I love this country and what it stands for."

These days, Bette is in the middle of a novel that she's been working on for quite a long time. "I find myself taking it apart, putting it together, taking it apart, putting it together. If I have anything to tell anybody about writing, it's that it's a long process. Writers spend most of their time revising what they've written, over and over again. It's a craft that requires a great deal of patience and distance from your own work."

In her mind, Bette has what she calls a "hat rack" for each writing project. "I have a lot of hats, which are facts or feelings or things I want to say. They are all bunched around. They are different colors. I don't know what to do with them. I need to find myself a hat rack. Once I find the hat rack, I can place the hats where they belong." As soon as she finds her "hat rack," she says, "it becomes the spine of my thinking."

When she gets stuck, Bette goes to sleep. "It's not magical, but sometimes you're trying so hard to work yourself out of a situation you've written yourself into, and you have no idea logically how you will jump out of that corner." Occasionally, after sleeping, says Bette, the answer pops out. "People tell me it's because I wasn't thinking about it."

For those who want to be writers, Bette has this advice: "Start." She finds that the most difficult sentence is the first sentence. "It seems to set the tone or get you ready to go."

For those who don't like to write, Bette says, "I would think it would be easier to tell your story to somebody. If you're having a terrible time with an assignment, tell it to your mother, or father, or brother, or sister, and see if you can make sense out of it by speaking about it."

Bette enjoys being a writer. "Everything I learn is something I can use. There are not too many fields like that. Every minute of your life can go into your writing—the boring parts, the frightening parts, the joyful parts, all of that." For that reason, *In the Year of the Boar and Jackie Robinson* is very special to Bette. "It really is an expression of love for what this country is and for my teachers and for that little school, P.S. 8."

> "To tell stories from my childhood, I had to write in the voice of a child."

DO IT YOURSELF!

Here is a writing activity from Bette Bao Lord: "When my son was young, I read him *Charlotte's Web*. At the end of the book, he was so sad, so undone, he asked me to rewrite the ending. I think that may be a fine exercise. Choose a book you like, with characters that stick in your mind, and rewrite the book's ending."

Janet Lunn

BORN: December 28, 1928, in Dallas, Texas
HOME: Hillier, Ontario, Canada

SELECTED TITLES

The Twelve Dancing Princesses
1979

The Root Cellar
1983

Double Spell
1985

Shadow in Hawthorn Bay
1986

Amos's Sweater
1988

Duck Cakes for Sale
1989

One Hundred Shining Candles
1991

◇

Janet Lunn thinks that all of her books are basically about the same thing. "What I always write about is traveling, never quite belonging, never being sure." She likes to feel, as a writer, that she's communicated with her readers. "I like to touch something, to strike a chord."

She believes that a fiction writer leads a double life—partly in the world of here and now and partly in the world that's being created. Most writers, she believes, don't anticipate all of the effects that their work will have on their readers. "I think that what moves you in art isn't always articulated by the artist," says Janet. "A person who sees or reads my work is quite often touched by something I didn't even realize I was putting in the work. When that happens to me, I feel that I've communicated with my reader. I've touched somebody else. I've hit a note and struck a chord." Janet feels the same way when she looks at beautiful paintings. "I love Picasso's paintings and can't tell you why. I am always drawn to a painting by Picasso. Something that he paints touches something in me. That's all I know."

Rewriting is a big part of Janet's process. "I rewrite an awful lot. I always rewrite six or eight times." She adds, "When I sew a seam, if it isn't right, I pull out the seam until there's not enough left to work on." Her perfectionism is a trait that she shares with the French painter Pierre Bonnard. "When he was an old man whose pictures hung in the Louvre, he went in with his friends and fixed his paintings."

Janet writes with a typewriter. "I type with very wide margins, and then I write all over the back. My manuscripts are as much handwritten as typed." She thinks that sometimes writing done on a computer is not as good as writing done on a typewriter. "It seems to me you can just push it through the computer without pushing it through your own set of feelings," she explains.

PLUNGING INTO THE PAST
Because Janet writes mainly historical fiction, one of the most time-consuming parts of her writing process is the research phase. "The research for historical fiction is sometimes harder than the research for historical nonfiction. There are all sorts of obscure things you have to find out. For instance, how did people in 1865 hang their clothes out to dry?"

Janet believes that accuracy is extremely important. "If you're not accurate, you can't convey the feeling of going back in time."

Now and then, Janet gets stuck as she's writing, especially if she feels that her concept of one of her characters is slipping. She sits down and writes the character's biography. The biography may become part of the story. Other times when she's stuck, Janet irons her big tablecloths. "The action of the iron seems to help."

"I live so much inside my stories when I'm working on them. I have a real mourning period when I'm finished."

◇

Janet lives in an old farmhouse, which was the setting for *The Root Cellar*. In that book, a contemporary girl found ghosts from the 1860s living in a house she'd just moved into. Janet is pretty sure that her own house is haunted. Her late husband claimed he saw the ghost. "And he heard her sing once, in the kitchen. He was home alone, but he thought I was making tea in the kitchen. By the time he got there, the singing had stopped." After they had moved into the house, which had been uninhabited for 20 years, they learned that everybody in the neighborhood believed it was haunted.

When she writes, Janet has strong pictures in her mind. "I'm not comfortable writing about a place where my feet haven't been. When I wrote *Shadow in Hawthorn Bay*, I went twice to the north of Scotland, just to walk around the countryside."

As a child, Janet was more of a daydreamer than a writer. She enjoyed reading the works of E. Nesbit and Louisa May Alcott. She also loved *Heidi*. But her favorite book in all the world is *The Secret Garden*. She still loves to read, especially the work of Canadian writers like Alice Munroe and Michael Ondaatje.

Janet's advice for those who like to write is to study a favorite writer and notice how he or she handles a situation. "One book I always use in workshops is *Charlotte's Web,* because it's so beautifully written."

To those who don't like to write, Janet recommends that they at least try to be literate and articulate. She thinks that too often students are encouraged to write fiction, as though that were the only way to develop their imaginations. In her opinion, that's not necessary. "Everybody's got an imagination," she says. "They just don't all work in the same way." Janet thinks there are all kinds of ways to write and that no one way is more important than another. "Why not learn to write a readable letter or a good essay?" she suggests.

The ROOT CELLAR

Janet Lunn

DO IT YOURSELF!

Here is a writing activity from Janet Lunn: "Continue this story: Alice went out of the house very early in the morning, and there was a girl sitting on the swing under the big chestnut tree. As she walked closer, the girl disappeared."

Kevin Major

BORN: September 12,1949, in Stephenville, Newfoundland
HOME: Newfoundland, Canada

SELECTED TITLES

Once Kevin Major was asked by a student how he got the confidence to know that what he had written was good enough to be published. Kevin replied, "The confidence came from within myself. I had read quite a number of books written about young people and had worked with teenagers a lot. I felt pretty sure that if what I had written was honest enough, it would be of interest to them."

Before he writes a book, Kevin does a fair amount of work getting his characters clear in his mind and setting out a plot line that will take the book from beginning to end—"not in a tremendous amount of detail, but enough to know pretty well what is going to happen before I start the actual writing of the book."

The number of rewrites he does depends on the book. In some cases, it seems to flow pretty well. "I may be confident after the first draft, but I usually do go into a second draft and a third draft at least." Sometimes he'll write a book without doing any work in advance. He just moves forward with an idea to see how to get it to work, without plotting it out too much beforehand. A new book of his, *Diana: My Autobiography*, was written that way. "It's about a girl who's fascinated with royalty, who has been reading the recent biography about Diana, Princess of Wales, and who is stirred over the summer months to write her own biography."

Kevin likes to complete the first draft of a manuscript and let it sit for

two or three months. He believes that this gives him a better perspective. He also likes to let his finished books sit for a while, before sending them to the publisher. "But that's not always feasible if I'm trying to meet a publishing deadline. I have to work within those parameters."

Kevin has written in a number of different settings. He now lives in the city of St. Johns in Newfoundland, Canada, where he writes in a basement study. "It's got a nice picture window that looks out over a park." Behind the park is a brewery. "So the view is part rustic and part industrial," says Kevin.

EVERY PICTURE TELLS A STORY

As Kevin's characters develop, he starts getting pictures of them in his mind. Sometimes he finds photographs that help him see what his characters might look like. "I'm working on a book set during World

War I," says Kevin. "I have pictures of officers and people engaged in the war. The pictures are taped to the wall above my writing space and I refer to them as I write."

"Most of what I've learned about writing is from reading."

When he gets stuck, Kevin most often sits down and rereads what he's written. "If I'm really stuck, I go back several chapters, to the beginning of the book, to try to get the flow going again, to see what misdirection I've taken." Sometimes, Kevin feels, being stuck means he's not meant to write what he's just written. "If there's some unevenness in the flow, maybe I've taken a turn in the narrative I should not have taken. When this happens, I try to regain a sense of the story and go with it." He doesn't think he's ever had writer's block, though he's quick to admit that "certain parts are much easier to write than others. It's just a matter of putting my mind in the right frame."

Kevin has also tried some playwriting. He has adapted his books *Hold Fast* and *Far From Shore* for the stage. He prefers novel-writing to stage-writing, all in all. "You're more your own person, doing your own thing, putting your own stamp on it," he says. Working as a playwright has its limitations. "Actors and directors get drawn into the process, and the story becomes a collaboration. You also have to consider the logistics of getting certain scenes on the stage." Writing a novel, Kevin feels, is a much freer experience. "You can go any place, any time." On the other hand, he loves the immediate reactions that you get from an audience in a theater. "When it works, it's a tremendous feeling. It's nerve-wracking when it doesn't."

Kevin is the youngest of seven children. As a child, he lived in a very small town with "not much of a library." He remembers not having access to as many books as he would like to have had. These days he reads a lot, but he admits that "like a lot of people, I have a very large collection of books that I've yet to find time to read."

Kevin used to be a teacher and still enjoys talking with kids. He finds that some kids who are interested in writing are anxious to get published. "I tell them that very few people get published until they're well into their twenties, or maybe later. It's a long, involved, difficult process, going from wanting to be a writer to getting published. But he also tells them, "If you are really, truly writers, the work will eventually come forth."

DO IT YOURSELF!

Here is a writing activity from Kevin Major: Write a letter to a person you admire. It could be someone you know or a famous person you see on TV. It doesn't matter whether you mail it or not—the process of writing it will be a rewarding experience! Why not try it?

Ann M. Martin

BORN: August 12, 1955, in Princeton, New Jersey
HOME: New York, New York

SELECTED TITLES

Bummer Summer
1983

Stage Fright
1984

*Me and Katie
(the Pest)*
1985

*Missing Since
Monday*
1986

*The Baby-Sitters
Club series*
1986–

Ma and Pa Dracula
1989

Ten Kids, No Pets
1989

*The Baby-Sitters'
Little Sisters series*
1989–

*Eleven Kids, One
Summer*
1991

*Rachel Parker,
Kindergarten
Show-off*
1992

*The Baby-Sitters
Club Mysteries*
1992–

◇

When Ann M. Martin was a girl, she ran a library in her bedroom for all the children in her neighborhood. She used her own books, and even charged fines for overdue books! Today, she still sets up libraries, through a foundation she helped establish called the Lisa Novak Community Libraries. "It was started in memory of a publishing friend," says Ann. "All we do is ask publishing companies to donate new books that are sitting around their offices. We gather them up, sort them into libraries, send them to homeless shelters, after-school programs, and camps for disadvantaged kids. It's a simple idea, but it's growing." Ann runs another foundation, too, called the Ann M. Martin Foundation. "We help organizations in three different areas," says Ann. "We help homeless people, education and literacy projects, and children."

Helping other people has always been part of Ann's life. She was raised to believe in good works and social responsibility. "There was a sense that everyone is as important as you are, that you can make a difference," Ann remembers. This attitude is very important to Ann, and it has been stressed in her writing. "The girls in the *Baby-Sitters Club* books have positive images, positive moral values, positive self-esteem," says Ann. "They are active in their community. They are responsible." Ann believes it's important for people—"and that includes kids"—to be involved and to know they can help others, "whether by donating money, or, more importantly, donating time and energy and ideas—their own personal talents. We all live in this world together. It's not only necessary, but it's fun to pitch in and help out in all kinds of ways. People can do that."

Ann grew up in Princeton, New Jersey, in a family that included her father, Henry Martin, an artist and cartoonist for *The New Yorker* magazine, her mother, Edie Martin, a former preschool teacher (Edie's maiden name, Matthews, is Ann's middle name), and a younger sister, Jane. Her childhood, Ann remembers, was "pretty wonderful." She thinks back on family outings, magic lessons, friendships, and big family art projects. It was also a childhood filled with books, many of which Ann still owns and looks at frequently. Some of her favorites include *A Cricket in Times Square* by George Selden, the *Mary Poppins* books by P. L. Travers, the *Mrs. Piggle-Wiggle* books by Betty MacDonald, the *Dr. Dolittle* books by Hugh Lofting, and, especially, Marguerite Henry's books about horses.

Ann is a very disciplined worker. She has to be. At any given time, she's usually working on three books: one book for *The Baby-Sitters Club* series, one for *The Baby-Sitters' Little Sisters* series, and one nonseries book (she has written 13 of these). One of her editors has called Ann "the hardest-working person I know."

"I was at a book signing once. A girl came up to me and asked: 'Do you know what the M. in your name stands for?'"

◇

Now that the series books are keeping her so busy, Ann doesn't have as much time as she'd like to write the nonseries books. "If I find myself with a free hour in the day, I'll work on one of the nonseries books," she says. "Sometimes I work on those types of books while I'm on vacation—then I have big blocks of free time." Some vacation!

Every morning, Ann gets up at 5:30, feeds her cats Mouse and Rosie, does other things around her house, and sits down to work at 8:30. She writes in the morning and edits in the afternoon. Ann writes with a fountain pen on lined paper, but not in any particular spot. "I move around from room to room, depending on who else is here," says Ann. She has two assistants who are in and out of her home during the week. Among other tasks, they help her answer her fan mail. Ann gets over 14,000 letters a year and sees to it that they all are answered. "This makes a difference to kids," Ann says. It's easy to see that she feels a great responsibility to her readers. "When I go to book signings, kids produce the letters we've sent back to them," says Ann proudly.

Ann gets ideas for her books from her own experiences, and from newspapers, magazines, and brainstorming sessions with her editors. For each book she writes, she begins with what she calls a "framework outline." Then she does a chapter-by-chapter outline. "So by the time I begin writing a manuscript, there's quite a bit to work with. It's hard for me to go astray when working from a chapter-by-chapter outline." When the outline is complete, she shows it to her editor, who makes comments. "Some of the editing is, in a sense, done ahead of time when the editor is looking at the outline," says Ann.

Her editors are often involved in devising plots for *The Baby-Sitters Club* books. "It's a collaborative process involving a lot of brainstorming," says Ann. "I don't do all of this entirely on my own." Though she no longer writes all of the books in *The Baby-Sitters Club* series, she has written about 75 percent of them and does the plotting and some editing for all of them.

Ann knows the characters in *The Baby-Sitters Club* series very well. "The nice thing about writing a series is that the characters have a better and better chance to develop," she says. After so many books, "the characters themselves are generating their own plot ideas."

In her spare time, Ann likes visiting with her friends and sewing clothes for children. She is fond of animals, especially cats. She also enjoys gardening and reading, especially children's books that have won Newbery Medals.

APPLE PAPERBACKS

Scholastic
0-590-43388-1 / $3.25 US / $3.95 CAN

#1

THE BABY SITTERS CLUB

Four friends and baby-sitting—what could be more fun?

Kristy's Great Idea

Ann M. Martin

SCHOLASTIC

DO IT YOURSELF!

Here is a writing activity from Ann M. Martin: Write a story based on this idea: "What if you woke up in the morning and discovered you were the only person left in the world?"

Norma Fox Mazer

BORN: May 15, 1931, in New York, New York
HOME: New York, New York

The best thing Norma Fox Mazer ever heard a kid say about writing was when she was talking to a 12-year-old boy about the difference between books and movies. The boy said, "I like books better than movies because in books, you walk beside the characters." Norma likes to think of her readers that way, as walking beside her characters while they read her stories.

Norma's writing process is, as she describes it, "muddly and messy." She never knows what's going to spark a story. "Stories have sprung from as small an event as my driving past an old trailer every day for months." That event was the starting point of a short story she wrote called "Chocolate Pudding," which is in her collection *Dear Bill, Remember Me?* She also does a lot of clipping from newspapers, but she rarely uses those stories. "They molder in my file," she says. "They are like my security blanket. I've always worried about running out of stories, although, by now, I know that's absurd. There are more stories I want to write than I will ever have time for."

OVERCOMING FEAR AND TERROR

Norma used to take a lot of notes before beginning to write. She doesn't do that as much any more. "Experience *has* made a difference," she says. "In the beginning I lacked confidence in myself. I often wrote in a state of fear and terror. I wanted so much to be a writer, and I didn't know if I was any good." While she was working on *A Figure of Speech*, her second book, she wrote 200 pages before she wrote a single page she would consider using in the book.

These days, as she's getting ready to begin a new story, she daydreams the story. She writes down phrases and fragments of scenes that come to her. "Sometimes I start writing before I should, before I know what my story is about. But the scenes in my head are insistent. They need to be put down."

Keeping focused, she says, is one of the hardest things about writing. "Thinking isn't easy. To think well takes discipline. I tend to drift off into my imagination. Imagining a scene is so wonderful—there's a temptation to let that take the place of thinking."

Early on, Norma writes down whatever she knows about the story she wants to tell. This helps her see what she doesn't know. She asks herself questions about every aspect of the story. "The best thing you can do to work out a story is to ask yourself questions about it. The key question for plotting is *And then what happened?* This is always what we want to know when we hear or read a story. Writing any story can be seen as a process of answering a series of questions."

"The act of having somebody else read my work helps me switch gears. I'm no longer so involved."

When Norma is ready to draft, she sits down at the computer, closes her eyes, and starts typing. "I put a hat on—an old fedora—and pull it down over my eyes. I don't want to look at the words. I want to look at what's in my mind. I see a scene, and I try to put down what I'm seeing, how people are standing, how the room is furnished, or what the weather is like if they're outdoors. I want to see how they say the words they say, what they do with their bodies, if they're carrying a newspaper or tying their shoelaces."

She hasn't always worked this way. When she used to write on a typewriter, she didn't find the hat or closing her eyes necessary. "But a computer screen, unlike a sheet of paper rolling out of the typewriter, is in my face, staring at me," she says.

In the first draft, she gives herself permission to write without punctuation or attention to grammar or spelling. "I tell myself I'm not writing, I'm just blatting. I take away the fearful idea that I have to do it right, or do it well. I let myself be sloppy and playful. It's like playing with mud. You're making something, but you're not trying to make a wonderful sculpture."

What's most important to her is to get words down, to capture scenes and dialogue. "The terrifying thing about writing is having nothing there to work on, to have it all waiting in my head," she says. "I'm not the kind of writer who can figure everything out beforehand."

Sometimes, though, she gets stuck. "Isn't that part of being a writer?" she asks. Then she may turn to her husband, Harry, who is also a writer. "I spill out my doubts and fears, but I don't want him to say anything," she explains. "I just want him to listen, so I can whine about my problems. By the time I'm through with that, my mind is usually working again. Of course, if that doesn't work, just walking away from it all for a while is a good thing to do."

Norma has known she wanted to be a writer since she was 13. "Before that, I wanted to be a nurse. I wanted to have adventures." She taught herself to read when she was four. "I would read anything when I was a kid. We always had books in our house, but if I didn't have a book to read, I'd read the back of the cereal box." She remembers especially fondly a copy of *Gulliver's Travels* with beautiful illustrations. "I can still see Gulliver standing in the palm of the hand of a beautiful princess."

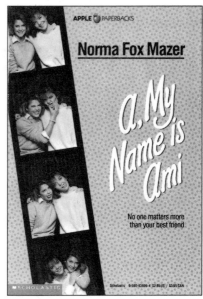

DO IT YOURSELF!

Here is a writing activity from Norma Fox Mazer: "For five minutes a day, write anything you want in a notebook. Write the first thing that comes to you. It could be something good that happened to you, or a fight you had. Or describe the contents of room, or a feeling, or how much you hate the fact that you agreed to do this exercise."

Ann McGovern

BORN: May 25, year unavailable, in New York, New York
HOME: New York, New York

W hen Ann McGovern gets ready to write a nonfiction book about one of her own real-life adventures, she keeps a diary of what she experiences. "Then I go into my eight- or nine-year-old excited mode," she explains, and she writes the book from the point of view of the child inside her who is having the adventure.

Ann has had lots of adventures. The author of more than 50 children's books, she has visited every continent on earth, from Africa to Antarctica. She has even been to the North Pole! She has written many books about the sea because of her love of scuba diving.

Ann started scuba diving in the early 1970s, soon after she married Marty Scheiner, who had three teenage children. Ann herself had a teenage son from a previous marriage. Marty said to Ann, "Let's try scuba diving." Ann recalls. "I said, 'Let's not,' because I'm a coward." Ann remembers sitting on a beach, holding her family's towels and suntan lotion, while they scuba dived. "Everybody came back sputtering with excitement," Ann says. "That did it." She had to try scuba diving herself. "I swallowed my fear and about half the ocean. I went down 80 feet on my first dive, and I thought I had died and gone to heaven." She was inspired by the beauty of the fishes and corals, and also, she remembers, "I had never felt so at home anywhere." After that experience, Ann wrote her first book about the ocean, *The Underwater*

World of the Coral Reef. She has since written many books about the ocean and its creatures.

DIVING IN

One of Ann's best-known books about the ocean, *Sharks*, was written after she saw a shark while she was diving. "It didn't gobble me up or bite my toe or do any of the things that sharks are supposed to do," she remembers. The harmless shark interested Ann so much that she decided to research and write a book about sharks. "I found out that most sharks are harmless," she said. While doing research for *Sharks*, Ann met Dr. Eugenie Clark, a world-renowned expert on sharks, and learned about Eugenie's fascinating adventures. She asked Eugenie if she could write a book about her. Eugenie laughed: "Oh, everybody says that." Ann wrote *Shark Lady: The True Adventures of Eugenie Clark.*

Since then, Ann and Eugenie have dived together often. They have gone on expeditions to save a coral reef in the Red Sea. They were among the first Americans to scuba dive in China. Ann has also dived with Eugenie in Indonesia and in the Caribbean. "Most of these expeditions were to study sharks and little fishes that disappear into the sand," says Ann. Those fish became the inspiration for the book *Desert Beneath the Sea*, which Ann wrote with Eugenie. "Children are fascinated with how a marine biologist works," Ann explains.

"After all these many books, I still over-research."

◇

After Ann had dived for 10 or 12 years, somebody asked her if she had ever tried night diving. This idea scared Ann at first, but she went anyway, and she's glad. Those experiences formed the basis for her book *Night Dive*.

When Ann sits down to write, there are certain rituals she follows: "Tearing my hair. Sharpening pencils. Eating." Ann describes herself as a compulsive writer, who wakes up early in the morning, before the phone rings. She takes a walk and starts writing when she comes home. Ann has two homes, one in the country and one in New York City. At her country house, she writes next to a window that looks out on a Japanese garden she calls "The Island of Quiet Meditation." Often she sees deer in that garden. "It's so beautiful, it's almost distracting." She's pushed her desk against the wall, so she "can concentrate and focus inwardly."

Though Ann travels a lot, she always finds time to visit schools in the United States and around the world.

Ann had a difficult childhood. Her father died when she was a baby. She remembers herself as "very sad and stuttering and lonely and miserable." Reading usually helped her feel better. "Books were my only answer, my only remedy and joy." Ann says she read to escape and she wrote about her feelings. "I loved poetry and stories. Always sad stories."

Ann has advice for those who like to write. "Keep a journal. Turn off the television and pick up a good book." She also suggests, "Don't be afraid of rewriting your stories many times. I rewrite each of my stories at least 25 times."

Ann stresses that feelings and curiosity are just as significant to a writer as great adventures. "You don't have to know how to scuba dive or travel around the world to be a writer," she says. "Everything that you want to write about is in you—what you're interested in, your family, and most important, your honest feelings."

SHARK LADY
TRUE ADVENTURES OF EUGENIE CLARK

by Ann McGovern

DO IT YOURSELF!

Here is a writing activity from Ann McGovern: "Complete this story: You put on all your scuba equipment and your heavy tank. You know that in a few minutes, you're going to be weightless under the sea. You jump into the sea and…." What happens next? Sharpen your pencil and write about it!

Robin McKinley

BORN: November 16, 1952, in Warren, Ohio
HOME: Hampshire, England

Robin McKinley has learned not always to rely upon her first impressions. Once she was giving a talk to a library group. A boy about 11 years old came in late, with his mother. He sat in a corner by himself. "He looked vague and arrogant, not interested in being where he was, as though he had better things to do. I was talking about the magical power of the Damarian people. [Those are the people who populate her books *The Blue Sword* and *The Hero and the Crown*.] I was describing this magical power as being something the people don't understand, that they don't know why they've got it, or what it can do. They can just tell the energy is there." The boy in the corner spoke up: "You're talking about the writing process, aren't you?" Robin liked that question—a lot. "I had to revise my estimate about this child," she says.

Robin writes because a story that wants to be written won't let her sleep unless she cooperates. She realizes that not everybody writes with this sense of the story holding the writer by the scruff of the neck. Robin is married to the writer Peter Dickinson, who has a very different method. "He sits down every morning at his manual typewriter and bangs out a couple of pages." Robin, on the other hand, tends to write "in bursts." As a result, she says, "he turns out books far more regularly than I do."

She writes the first draft of each book in longhand. During that part of the process, there are places where she has to stop. "I don't exactly come to the end of the story, but to the end of my energy." She puts down her pen or pencil and waits for her energy to build again. This starting and stopping also happens sometimes when she's writing her first typed draft. "By the time I'm in my third draft, which is usually the final draft I send to the publisher, there's been an increasing momentum. I hurtle along. I'm desperate to get to the end." After she finishes her third draft, she usually sends it out. "Since by then it's usually horrendously late, I have to send it out to convince people I haven't died."

AN AMERICAN ABROAD

Though Robin is American, she has been living in England for several years. She says, "I like it fine. It seems like quite a good idea." Robin admits that she's always had what she calls a "rose-colored glasses crush" on England. "My favorite authors from when I was a little kid have always been English." (Three of these English writers are Rudyard Kipling, J. R. R.

Tolkien, and Peter Dickinson, a favorite long before she met and married him.)

Since moving to England, Robin's become an avid gardener. She lives and works in a "big old rambling English country house with huge rooms that are impossible to keep warm." Her workroom is at one end of a drawing room, which has enormous French doors that open out onto a garden. Her desk faces bookshelves and a lot of old horse statues. She says, "If my desk faced into the garden, I'd never get any work done." The workroom is also filled with CDs, because Robin plays music constantly while she works.

"One of my consistent rules for a workroom is don't have a view, because you'll look at it."

Robin says she imagines everything that happens in her books "at some point along the way." Sometimes, she'll get a picture in her head before she knows what story it belongs to. For example, her novel *The Blue Sword* grew from an image she kept seeing in her imagination of a woman standing on a mountain bringing the sky down to fall on the heads of enemies, who were too strong for her. That the enemies were too strong is a crucial aspect of the image. The woman was pulling the sky down with a blue sword. Eventually, Robin was able to discover the story that went along with that powerful image.

Robin takes long walks every day with her husband and their three whippets. This is especially helpful when she gets stuck in her writing. "As we walk, often Peter thinks about his story, and I think about mine." Sometimes they talk out their writing problems as they walk. "We can talk to each other about our stories more easily than we can talk to anybody else."

As a child, Robin wrote fragments of stories. She remembers having "great beginnings, great endings, and no middles to stick them together." By the time Robin was 18 years old, she had finished "a few short stories, quite a few poems, and one extraordinarily bad novel."

If you want to be a writer, says Robin, "Keep writing. Keep reading. Don't let anybody bully you." If you don't want to be a writer, Robin says, that's fine too. "We have more writers than we need at this point. What we need are good car mechanics."

DO IT YOURSELF!

Here is a writing activity from Robin McKinley: "Add a chapter to a favorite book. I'm always making up the bits that the writer didn't put in. That's why I'm a slow reader." Where would you add the chapter? In the middle? At the end? Would you change the end of a favorite story? When you try to do that, you might get some insight into the reasons the author chose to end the book the way he or she did.

Patricia McKissack

BORN: August 9, 1944, in Nashville, Tennessee
HOME: Clayton, Missouri

SELECTED TITLES

Paul Laurence Dunbar, a Poet to Remember
1984

The Incas
1985

Mary McLeod Bethune: A Great American Educator
1985

The Maya
1985

Flossie and the Fox
1986

A Long Hard Journey: The Story of the Pullman Porter
1989

Frederick Douglass: A Leader Against Slavery
(with Frederick McKissack)
1991

Louis Armstrong: Jazz Musician
1991

The Dark-Thirty: Southern Tales of the Supernatural
(Newbery Honor Book)
1992

Sojourner Truth: Ain't I a Woman?
(with Frederick McKissack)
1992

Patricia McKissack writes both fiction and nonfiction. She writes nonfiction mostly in partnership with her husband, Frederick. Is there a difference between writing fiction and nonfiction? "Believe it," says Pat. "Apples and oranges."

Pat approaches fiction writing with "the child in me that has never died, thank goodness." She enjoys letting the child within her write about things she feels she was denied. "I was denied a book about a little girl who was my color, who had experiences similar to my own. I didn't even find a white child who was like me."

Asked how long it takes her to write a fiction story, Pat answers, "About one year to work it through my head, and two weeks to write it." During the year she's got the story in her head, Pat sees pictures moving. "I see the people talking and doing stuff." She urges the child's voice inside her head to talk, to describe what's going on. "I let the child tell me what's interesting and what's not." Pat never worries about losing the story she carries around in her head for so long. "If I lost it, it wasn't there in the first place."

DETAILS MAKE THE DIFFERENCE

When the McKissacks write nonfiction, they feel a strong sense of responsibility. "We [nonfiction writers] have to bring information to young readers in an interesting way,

and not turn them off from knowing who they are and where they've come from," says Pat. She wants readers of nonfiction books to pick up those books "with the exact same enthusiasm and expectations of a good read as a fiction book."

As Fred and Pat study somebody they want to write about, they try to look for fun facts that will spark their readers' interest. For example, Pat says when they were researching the life of poet Paul Laurence Dunbar, they discovered that he walked to school with inventors Orville and Wilbur Wright and that he took his bicycle to their shop for repair. "When you find stuff like that, you just twitch. Like a cat at a window who sees a yummy morsel," says Pat.

Pat and Fred's aim in writing biographies is to "bring these people to life and let them breathe and smell and taste." Pat feels that many biographies written for children lack texture. "Too often, they are flat and one-dimensional. I like to put my subjects in the world where they were." For example, Pat says if they were writing about somebody who went to New York City in 1773 and worked for seven years, "I would want my readers to know there were still big ships bringing in slaves then. I would want my readers to smell the smells of the town, to hear wagons clattering over cobblestones, and the cries of people selling bread from baskets, and the streets teeming with life. I would want them to feel the mosquitoes."

"When writing nonfiction, you have to make sure to throw out what you can't prove."

◇

Pat and her husband decided to become writers after each had reached a "glass ceiling" in their previous jobs. "Fred had his own company. He was working night and day, and not seeing a whole lot of progress. He was losing his hair and losing his life, he was so full of stress," remembers Pat. "I was the same way. Walking up the walls. One night, we were just talking and he said to me, 'If you could do anything in the world you wanted to do, what would it be?' I said I'd always wanted to write books for children. He said, 'You know what? You don't come around but once. This is not a dress rehearsal. Go write. I'll go with you as far as you can go.' I said, 'Do you mean it?'" He did.

It took five years for the new venture to succeed. "Five very lean and hard years. We have wonderful sons who understood. They accepted the lean Christmases and no vacations. They rallied around us. They worked with us."

Pat claims she never gets writer's block. "Honey, I owe too many bills to get blocks," she says. "Blocks are for people who have the luxury of melodrama. I don't have time. I have to pay bills. So please let me tell you, when I get a block, I go find something else very quickly to work on. I don't block. I switch."

As a child, Pat made up stories all the time and played by herself hour after hour. "My parents would observe me and ask each other, 'Is the child all right?'" She pretended to be a ballerina, a scout, an ice skater. "I have skated more concerts on grass!"

Pat grew up in Nashville, Tennessee where, as a young African-American, there were many places, like hotels, parks, and even concert halls, where she was not permitted to go. But the doors were always open to one building that became very important to her. "Nashville's public libraries were not segregated," she remembers. "We could get books. The librarians smiled and treated me like a human being. That formed my attitude toward books and libraries and librarians. I have a love and a loyalty to them. They opened up a world to me I otherwise wouldn't have had."

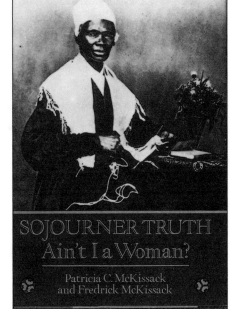

DO IT YOURSELF!

Here is a writing activity from Patricia McKissack: "Find a family story and write about it. Get your mother to tell you something that happened when she was a little girl. Ask your father to talk about something that happened to him when he was a child. Or ask your grandmother, or your aunt. Listen to their voices as they talk to you. Listen to their language patterns. Pull a story from those family experiences. It's a rich and wonderful way of preserving that part of you that comes to you through your family."

Phyllis Reynolds Naylor

BORN: January 4, 1933, in Anderson, Indiana
HOME: Bethesda, Maryland

Over a period of months or usually years, whenever Phyllis Reynolds Naylor gets an idea about a particular book, she writes it down in a notebook specially set aside for that book. She has a shelf of these notebooks in the room where she works. The notebooks have pockets in them to hold relevant magazine articles, photographs that remind Phyllis of one of the book's characters, maps of the area, or pages from the area's phone book. This collecting and note-taking usually goes on for a year or two before Phyllis is ready to begin writing the book. "I know I'm ready to start writing the book when I begin waking early in the morning, thinking about it. I'm excited. I can't wait to get going."

Whichever book excites her in that way is the one she writes next. "By that time, the material in that notebook may be an inch or two thick, with summaries, character sketches, climactic scenes, themes, or other things I want to include." She sits down and looks through the notebook. "What's in there is sometimes more wonderful than I'd remembered, or not as wonderful. It's like opening a box of surprises."

Children's novels don't take Phyllis as long to write as adult novels. (She writes both.) That is simply because they're not as long. "It's not the writing that takes the time. It's the thinking," she says. "That is so hard to get across to students. From the time I sit down with my notebook and start to write until the time I send the manuscript to my editor may be from three to six months. But I may have been thinking about the book for two years before I started writing it."

Getting stuck is not a real problem for Phyllis. "I've usually thought through my story well," she says. Sometimes, she'll notice that her writing may have gone flat for a couple of pages. If that happens, "I just stop, either for the day or for a few hours." She'll occasionally take a three-mile walk to think the problem through, which is how she usually starts her day, anyway. "I generally give myself a writing problem before I begin my walk," says Phyllis. "If I don't have a particular writing problem at that moment, I think about the next scene I'm going to write."

BECOMING A WRITER

When she speaks to groups of schoolchildren, Phyllis often tells them, "For those of you who are going to become writers, I have news for you. You have already begun." She likes to quote the writer Willa Cather, who observed that "the years between eight and 15 are the formative period in a writer's life." Phyllis's family always says to her, "You have such a memory for your childhood!" Phyllis assumes that everyone remembers their childhood. "The things I go back to—the fears, doubts, emotions, and injustices—are things that occurred to me between eight and 15," she says. "Children at that age become very interested in problems they're having with themselves or with their parents and friends. They're forming opinions about things, meeting all sorts of problems for the first time. These are making an indelible impression on them." If they become writers, says Phyllis, "these impressions will come out throughout the rest of their lives in writing."

"I can never seem to start writing a book until I know what the title is going to be."

These days, Phyllis is trying to devote some time to reading. "I like reading about very ordinary people in extraordinary situations," she says. "My feeling is that people with money and education and social know-how have so many advantages, that when they are faced with a problem, often the money or the education will solve it. But when, for example, a child in Appalachia faces a problem [such as Marty Preston in Phyllis's Newbery Award-winning book *Shiloh*] it's a far greater problem to him. He has to be much more creative in solving the problem, because he doesn't necessarily have the social skills or the education or the money."

Phyllis likes going to plays and spending time with her family. She likes to travel too—somewhat. "I

really sometimes think, when we go on a trip and are looking at the usual tourist sights, 'This is very nice, but I'm not doing anything with this. It's too passive.'" She likes being involved in a process all the time, in creating something. "Just passively traveling around the world looking at monuments and things doesn't send me as much as writing," admits Phyllis. "If I could press a button and in the next 15 minutes see the pyramids and be back home again, I'd do it. Getting there and back, when I could be writing a whole book in that time, seems like a waste to me."

Phyllis Reynolds Naylor, who has written so much already, clearly doesn't like to waste time. She has too many stories she's excited about telling.

DO IT YOURSELF!

Here is a writing activity from Phyllis Reynolds Naylor: "Look around the room. Write down what you would notice if you were a six-year-old child coming into that room. Then write down what you would notice if you were 20, 45, or 80 years old. You might start to notice that a small child's eye level is way down low. The child might look for a pet or for a candy dish or for bright colors. The 80-year-old might want to find a chair to sit in, away from drafts. This helps you get into the skin of the character you're writing about."

Joan Lowery Nixon

BORN: February 3, 1927, in Los Angeles, California
HOME: Houston, Texas

SELECTED TITLES

The Mysterious Red Tape Gang
1974

The Kidnapping of Christina Lattimore
1979

The Seance
1980

The Stalker
1985

Beats Me, Claude
1986

The House on Hackman's Hill
1986

A Family Apart (The Orphan Train Quartet series)
1987

The Other Side of Dark
1987

Fat Chance, Claude
1987

Haunted Island
1987

Whispers From the Dead
1989

Land of Hope
1992

The Weekend Was Murder
1992

When Joan Lowery Nixon sits down to write, it's as though the rest of the world slips away. "I lose track of time when I'm writing," she says. "Sometimes I come out of it and think, 'What day is this?'" Writing has been part of Joan's life almost since she learned how to speak. "My mother told me that at the age of two, before I was old enough to read or write, I would come to her and say, 'Write this down. I have a poem.'" She published her first magazine article when she was 17.

Before Joan starts to write a new book, she sometimes consults a file she keeps, which she calls her "bank account of ideas. In there, I put newspaper clippings, maybe a sentence or a couple of paragraphs I've jotted down. Sometimes I dump it all down on the bed and look through it, finding just what I'm looking for."

When Joan is about to start writing a new book, she sits at her desk "with a bit of fear." As the words roll around in her head, she worries, "Will I be able to say everything I want to say?" Sometimes she avoids getting right down to starting the story. "That's a good time to make a dental appointment," she says. "But usually I just push through the fear. By the third or fourth page, I'm at home."

Joan writes at a word-processor. "As I write, I rewrite," she explains. "I feel like a sculptor with a ball of clay, which I pinch and poke and push and mold. Sometimes I even squash my 'clay' all together and start over again." After a morning of "sculpting,"

Joan prints out a copy of her work. "I can think better about my work on paper rather than on the computer screen," she says. She goes over the printout, and the next morning, puts in the changes she's made.

Getting stuck is not a big problem for Joan, though she admits that some days "it feels like every word comes out of my head with a pair of pliers." Usually, by the time she starts to write a book, she has spent a lot of time thinking about what she will write. Sometimes, Joan has a problem that might be thought of as the *opposite* of writer's block. "Once in a while, I have a day when everything comes into my head so fast that I can't write it down quickly enough."

A HUNGRY READER

As a child, Joan "gobbled books." She remembers reading anything she could get her hands on. Particularly, she remembers *Little Women*. "I wanted to be Jo March. She had an attic to write in. I felt deprived. I had no attic." She also loved classics such as *The Five Little Peppers and How They Grew* and *The Railway Children*. Joan is glad to see that some children are still reading these books, which were written a very long time ago. "I have an 11-year-old granddaughter who was here last summer," says Joan. "I gave her *The Railway Children*, and after she read it, I asked her what she thought of it. She said she loved it! I asked her if she found it old-fashioned, and she said she didn't and that she loved the way the children in the book lived." Joan thinks the book may still be popular because it talks about a gentler era, which she thinks children like to know about.

"I started writing when my children were small. I pulled the playpen over to my typewriter."

To would-be writers, Joan suggests, "Don't think too much about getting published. Write for your own pleasure." Joan thinks that children should be encouraged to play with words and to make up poems and funny stories. She's glad that schools are encouraging children to write, because she believes this helps children love writing at an early age.

Joan has taught writing to many children and adults. Some of her students didn't really want to learn how to write, but she helped them understand how important it was for them to learn to express themselves. "You have to know how to write," she says. Though she believes that good writing techniques can be taught, Joan admits that not everyone learns the same way or at the same pace. "My daughter Kathy's best subject was

APPLE PAPERBACKS

Scholastic
0-590-42370-9 / $2.75 US / $3.95 CAN

THE HOUSE ON HACKMAN'S HILL

Joan Lowery Nixon

Everyone had told them to stay away.

English," says Joan. "But I could never get my daughter Maureen off roller skates or out of a tree. I'd say to her, 'Don't you like to read, sweetheart?' and she'd say, 'I do, and I would read a lot if I could read while I'm roller skating.'"

When teaching writing, Joan has always stressed the importance of a strong opening sentence, and using lots of action words. "Everyone has to learn techniques of communication," she says. "I think writing programs help everybody." There's satisfaction in teaching writing, Joan has found. "I could see the ones who had less talent improve," she recalls. "And those with talent shot right through the roof."

DO IT YOURSELF!

Here is a writing activity from Joan Lowery Nixon: "Write a short scene from your own viewpoint. Then pretend you're somebody very different. Write the same scene from that other person's point of view." Try it!

Daniel Pinkwater

BORN: November 15, 1941, in Memphis, Tennessee
HOME: Hudson County, New York

Daniel Pinkwater thinks that the question, "Where do you get your ideas?" is a bit silly. "Ideas come 60 a minute to everybody, not just me. And like everyone else's ideas, mine are mostly lousy." But he has learned how to work with his ideas. "I take one of those lousy ideas and chew on it, tug at it, and develop it until it starts to be a better sort of idea."

When Daniel starts to write anything, he uses what he calls "the greatest single and only formula for writing fiction: the two words *what if*. So, a kid is sent to the store. What if he's sent to the store to get the Thanksgiving turkey? What if they haven't got any birds of any kind? What if he ends up buying a 266-pound chicken? That's how ideas get developed. The next step is to develop the plot."

Once Daniel was giving a talk at a school. A kid looked him up and down and said, "You're not really the guy who wrote those books, are you?" Daniel thought the question showed insight and sensitivity. "He looked me over, he heard a few words from me, and he realized that I'm just another stupid adult—that I'm nothing like the guy who writes the books must be." Daniel thinks the kid was right. "He was meeting me in my adult persona. The only time my child persona comes out is when I'm alone at the computer. Even *I* find the actual me boring. But the one that does the writing is kind of clever." Daniel says that when he sits down to write, he

feels like he's meeting up with an old friend. "Or more than an old friend. I know it's me. Part of the pleasure of writing for an audience that is younger than I am is that I get to go back to a particular kid who is me, younger than I am."

A BUILT-IN AGE-APPROPRIATE CRITIC

He has thought his theory through well. "If you're eight years old and then you get to be nine, you don't stop being eight years old. Likewise, the nine-year-old is incorporated into the 10-year-old, and so on." When he sits down to write a children's book, he uses what he calls a "simple device. I go back and figure out what this nine-year-old would have read, or would like to read now. Then I write that book for him. I have a built-in age-appropriate critic to make sure I don't wander into writing about human relations or something boring."

In addition to many artifacts and

memorabilia, Daniel's office contains a desk and a big old leather couch with a dog on it. The dog, "a great monstrous brute," came home with Daniel from the pound, at which time he looked "like he was made out of pipe cleaners." Thanks to daily walks with his master, the dog is now a "tremendous athlete."

On Daniel's desk is a little statue of a Chinese man named Ho Chi. "He was a Chan master who threw it all over to walk around with a little bag of cookies. The kids all liked him because he gave them cookies. When he ran into an adult, they'd ask him to knock it off and be a teacher. He'd say, 'Give me a penny.' He's like me."

"All of my stories are based in Chicago in one apartment."

As a child, Daniel was "surprisingly happy" and a writer already. He remembers writing one-page parodies when he was in fifth grade. "I was highly inspired by *Mad* magazine," he recalls. "I bought the first issue off the newsstand." In school, Daniel used to write funny notes "that I would pass around the classroom to try to make my friends laugh out loud and get in trouble."

His breakthrough moment came when he entered a short-story contest in school and won a prize—a subscription to *National Geographic*. "That's how I first learned that you could get things by writing. It was a lesson I didn't dwell on, but I knew somewhere in my head that you could trade writing for things."

What does Daniel like to read these days? He answers, "I stopped." But he read a lot before he stopped. "The last thing I read was *Moby Dick*. I read it continuously for a period of 15 years.

Now I read it sporadically."

When not writing children's literature, Daniel says he likes to "think in my head." He enjoys writing and reading commentaries for National Public Radio. He's also endlessly interested by people. "I like to know people and witness the different things they work out and how they do it." He doesn't have too many friends near where he lives. "My neighbors stay away from me completely," says Daniel, which he likes. "It's very good for me in terms of preventing me from developing an inflated ego. Nobody knows what I do or could possibly care."

Once he allowed the local paper to interview him. "I was launching a syndicated comic strip," he explains, "and I was willing to do anything to get it publicized." After that, he was better known in town. "All the different citizens came up to me and said, 'So you do a cartoon!' They finally had an idea of what I did, this big, shambling man with a Woody Allen hat and a dog."

DO IT YOURSELF!

Here is a writing activity from Daniel Pinkwater: When Daniel writes a story, he asks the "nine-year-old who still lives inside him" what he would like to read. Try locating the six-year-old who still lives inside *you*. Write a story that the six-year-old would like to hear.

Doris Buchanan Smith

BORN: June 1, 1934, in Washington, D.C.
HOME: Canton, Missouri

SELECTED TITLES

A Taste of Blackberries
1973

Return to Bitter Creek
1986

Karate Dancer
1987

Kelly's Creek
1989

The First Hard Times
1990

Being a writer, Doris Buchanan Smith believes, is the experience of solitude. "When you write, you're alone. It is a solitary occupation." Once a child asked her, "Are you always so alone?" Doris thought that question was perceptive. She answered, "When I work I am, but I have other things going on in my life when I'm not working."

Sometimes events in Doris's books have surprised her. "I didn't know *A Taste of Blackberries* was going to be sad," she says. (That is Doris's well-known book that tells about the death of a young boy named Jamie.) "Though fiction writers use lots of made-up stuff, sometimes bits and pieces of real things pop into their heads, too." In the book, two best friends go to scrape Japanese beetles off a grapevine, which is something Doris remembers doing as a kid. As she wrote the scene, Doris kept the thought in her mind that the character Jamie was a cut-up. "I figured it was time for something funny to happen. I thought, 'What if they found a beehole and stuck a stick in it and ran shrieking home.' Now, if that happened to you, it's not funny, but when somebody else gets stung, it's comical." Doris remembers laughing at her typewriter as she was writing.

"Jamie always exaggerated everything," says Doris. "When he fell on the ground after he got stung, the idea popped into my head that he would die from the bee sting. I was absolutely shocked. I said, 'No. I'm not going to do that to Jamie.' But the idea

was insistent. It kept haunting me. So I did it." From that experience, Doris advises others to pay attention to those ideas that pop into their heads. "They may only be junk, but sometimes your best stories will come out that way."

There are two kinds of writers, Doris believes. "One kind thinks everything they write is wonderful. The other kind thinks everything they write is terrible." She thinks she's one of the former kinds of writers. "No matter how long I let the manuscript sit, for two weeks or two months, when I go back and look at it, it still looks wonderful to me. Objectivity is valuable, but I guess I still don't have enough of it!"

FEELING AT HOME

After living in Georgia for many years, Doris moved to northeast Missouri, to a house that overlooks the Mississippi River. Moving was a harder adjustment than she'd expected. "I hadn't moved in so long, I didn't remember what it was like. Other people are involved in their lives, and here you come." Her early time in her new home was also marred by two bad falls that she suffered soon after moving. "My life got to be like a Marx Brothers comedy," she laughs, and adds that she has now fully recovered.

On her desk, Doris has a lot of favorite things. "I have a Buddha who has his head tilted. He's a thinking Buddha. He's on top of my computer." Doris likes having pretty things around, a trait she says she gets from her mother, who was known to those in her family as "The Whatnot Queen of the World."

> **"Every one of my books wants to be as long as *War and Peace*. I always leave a lot of wonderful stuff on the cutting room floor."**

The hardest thing Doris ever had to learn as a writer was to become disciplined. "I wanted my writing to be art," she says. "I thought sitting down and working at it would ruin the art, which was a stupid idea. Many writers say they can't write until they get in the mood. I say, the first job is to get in the mood."

When she was still developing her habits of discipline, Doris had to invent some rituals that helped her settle down. "I would get a cup of English-style tea with hot milk. Then I would pick up a book in which I've underlined passages that are important to me." Books that she's underlined heavily include John Steinbeck's *A Life in Letters, Portrait of an Artist* by Laurie Lyle, *The Snow Leopard* by Peter Mathiesson, and Edward Abbey's *Desert Solitaire*. She still follows this procedure sometimes,

paging through one of these books, looking at passages she's underlined. Those important passages usually inspire her to begin writing.

Doris is a very visual person who loves writing where she can look out a window. "Some writers think looking out is too distracting, but I love it," she says. "Once I get going, it's like a bell jar comes over me anyway. I don't see the room or the window or anything."

Doris loved to write as a child. "I was probably a writer before I knew I was," she says. "When I was in sixth grade, I had a teacher who thought I had talent. She said, 'Do you want to be a writer?'" Doris was stunned. "Something in me said 'YEAH! That's what I want to do!'" She started writing then, whenever she had time or had an idea or was in the mood. "But that didn't get me anywhere," says Doris. "I kept hearing about discipline, that professional writers really work at it. I thought that meant hack writers. I didn't know then that you don't have any art without also having the craft."

If you want to be a writer, you might follow Doris's method: "I divide my writing into the creative thinking and the technical editing," she says. She puts the technical editing part in the corner and says, "Don't you dare come out until I'm ready." She lets herself write with no thought to grammar or spelling at first. "If there's nothing on the paper to practice your grammar or spelling on, what's the point?" Most of all, Doris lets herself enjoy the process and the end product. "I think the most wonderful thing is to have work that you love."

Doris Buchanan Smith

A Taste of Blackberries

> ## DO IT YOURSELF!
> Here is a writing activity from Doris Buchanan Smith: "Write a 1,000-word sentence. Don't worry about the ending. Just get your stream of consciousness going. If 1,000 words is too long for you, try writing a 200-word sentence. It's amazing what comes out."

Jerry Spinelli

BORN: February 1, 1941, in Norristown, Pennsylvania
HOME: Phoenixville, Pennsylvania

SELECTED TITLES

Space Station Seventh Grade
1982

Who Put that Hair in My Toothbrush?
1984

Night of the Whale
1985

Jason and Marceline
1986

Dump Days
1988

The Bathwater Gang
1990

Maniac Magee
(Newbery Medal)
1990

Fourth Grade Rats
1991

Report to the Principal's Office!
1991

There's a Girl in My Hammerlock
1991

Do the Funky Pickle
1992

Who Ran My Underwear up the Flagpole?
1992

Jerry Spinelli's favorite book of the many he's written is *Space Station Seventh Grade*, partly because it was his first published book. "You get sentimental about your first," he says. This book grew, in part, out of Jerry's family life. (He and his wife have reared six children.) "One morning I opened my refrigerator to get the fried chicken I had left there the night before. I was going to take it to work for my lunch. I looked in the bag. I saw bones, no chicken. Someone had eaten my chicken. I knew it was one of the six sleeping angels upstairs, but nobody would confess. I went to work fried chickenless."

At lunchtime, the chicken was still on Jerry's mind. "I was still mad about it and I started to write. I was about to write about it from my own point of view, when for some unknown, but as it turned out, blessed reason, it occurred to me that there was a more interesting point of view here, the point of view of the kid who took the fried chicken. So I started writing from the kid's point of view. The first paragraph in the book contains the very words I wrote that day, without a change. A lot of folks would have seen a bag of chicken bones. I saw a career."

In those days, Jerry worked full-time for a publishing company. Though it kept him from spending his days writing stories, the job was a necessity, because of the six children. Jerry finally quit when most of his children were grown because "I didn't want to come to the end of the line and look back and say, 'If I only had the guts to try.'"

WRITING DURING LUNCH BREAKS

Jerry admits that winning the Newbery Medal in 1991 helped. "Before that, I was one mortgage payment from bankruptcy." He wrote his Newbery award-winning book, *Maniac Magee,* during his lunch hours at work. "All my books up to then were written on lunch hours or on weekends."

Jerry knew he wanted to be a writer from the time he was 16 years old. "I didn't know how hard it would be, or how long it would take me." Finally, he is doing what he always wanted to do: making his living writing books.

His process is not too deliberate. "I'll just have an idea, which may have come from any source and may develop into a book. I don't try to be too calculating or measured or deliberate or organized about it at first." Jerry thinks that too much organization can cause a writer to lose a certain mental elasticity. He tries to put off his decision-making until the last minute, to prolong the formative stage of a book for as long as possible. "I like to let it be chaotic, so possibilities can reign and prevail. Out of that mess, gradually, hopefully, a story will begin to take shape."

"One of my goals in writing is to transmit the picture in my head to the reader—the reverse of what I do when I'm reading. When I'm reading, the picture comes to me."

Though he swears by his method, Jerry realizes that there are more orderly ways to write books. "Doing it my way, you end up with snags. I don't always know where I am going in my stories. Sometimes that can be frustrating." But there is an up side to this process: "It introduces spontaneity and fresh, unexpected elements to the story."

Unlike most authors, Jerry doesn't rewrite much. "I guess English teachers wouldn't like to hear me say that," he laughs. "I don't write the first draft and then practically throw it away, as I understand some authors do. I pretty much try to get it right the first time." After he writes a passage, he reads it aloud to himself the next day. "I think that reading aloud helps you detect things in the story that you might otherwise not notice."

How does he manage to avoid doing much rewriting? "Usually I don't write until I know what I want to write." Though he tries not to be too organized beforehand, he knows what

he wants to write in a general way. "I compare it sometimes to a fast break in basketball, getting a rebound at one end of the court. You know you want to go to the other end of the court and put the ball in the basket. You know where the hoop is, you know what you're going to do. You just don't know every move you will make along the way."

In some ways, Jerry sees the notion of writer's block as an indulgence. "Teachers don't wake up in the morning and say 'I have teacher's block.' Writers are the only ones who excuse themselves from their own occupation."

Though Jerry feels that writing is mostly a lot of hard work, he believes that once or twice he has been visited by a muse, an invisible spirit, that guided his hand as he wrote. The first time was when he realized that he should write his fried-chicken story from the point of view of the kid who stole the chicken. Another time was when he was starting to write *Maniac Magee.*

"I had made two or three false starts on that book," he remembers. "I didn't feel I had the voice right." He took a couple of days off to get away from it, hoping he would see it more clearly when he returned. When he sat down at his desk again, the words that opened the book came to him. "I don't feel as if I went out and got them. I had sort of put the book aside, mentally speaking. Then, as soon as I stopped looking for them, they visited me. They bit me."

To those who like to write, Jerry advises, "Write about what you care about. That's when you are going to do your best writing. The idea is to touch the reader. If you're not touching yourself, you're not going to touch the reader."

DO IT YOURSELF!

Here is a writing activity from Jerry Spinelli: "Come up with your own similes. Make them as outlandish and individual and creative as possible." "*Cheeks like roses*" is a simile and so is "sly as a fox," but they're not very exciting. That's where you come in. Follow Jerry's advice and write five to 10 super similes. When you're finished, put them in a story.

Joyce Carol Thomas

BORN: May 25, 1938, in Ponca City, Oklahoma
HOME: Caryville, Tennessee

SELECTED TITLES

Marked by Fire
1982

Bright Shadow
1983

The Golden Pasture
1986

Water Girl
1986

Journey
1988

A Gathering of Flowers: Stories About Being Young in America
(editor)
1990

Brown Honey and Broom Wheat Tea
1993

When the Nightingale Sings
1993

Joyce Carol Thomas lives without fear. "I saw a tornado recently," she says. "I was driving from Atlanta. I was about 20 miles from my home, traveling on a freeway. I saw a funnel with electric green light in it. The radio was saying there were tornadoes in the area. They rarely have tornadoes in this part of Tennessee. Back home in Oklahoma, the tornadoes came. I'm not afraid of them." Joyce has a car phone. One of her friends called on the car phone to see if she was all right. "I said, 'There's a tornado on my right,'" says Joyce. "I just kept on driving. I'm fascinated by acts of nature."

One reason Joyce is fearless is because, she says, "I'm living in the now." Joyce says that many people think they're above nature or that they can control it. But Joyce has a different belief: "We're all just part of the universe, part of everything. Tornadoes hit when the hit."

THE GIFT OF STORIES

Joyce has distinct views on writing too. "A lot of times, you'll hear about competition between this writer and that writer," she says. "I smile to myself. What you write is a gift. You write the best you can write. That's the joy of it." She calls the giver of this gift a spirit. "It's so much a part of me that I find myself listening for it and having it guide me to do the right thing, to write books that I hope will resonate for people. When it's present, I feel its guidance."

She rewrites each of her books at least 10 times. "That's because I keep going back and filling in more details," says Joyce. "When I tell students that I write 10 drafts, they gasp. I explain that writing is a process." Usually, English teachers come up after Joyce's talks and thank her for emphasizing that point. "Kids think you just sit down and write a book like you write a letter, and then it's over."

Joyce's editors are familiar with her process of filling in more details. She wrote a story called "Young Reverend Thelma Lee Moses" for *A Gathering of Flowers*, a multicultural anthology she assembled. Joyce sent the manuscript of her story to her editor. "Then I got some more details," she remembers, adding that she sent in four drafts in all. "My editor said to the associate editor, 'Put that draft in a drawer. There are more coming. This is the way a *real* writer works.'"

Joyce says, "This method works for me. Different people work in different ways. Nobody has to work the way I do. You don't have to write what I write. Write what's inside of you."

The window in Joyce's study looks out on a serene lake. As she writes, she watches bald eagles, red-tailed hawks, blackbirds, and great blue herons outside. "For me, looking out at the beauty of the lake is what makes the room special." She loves driving from nearby Knoxville to her home in the country, "knowing that I am coming to such a peaceful place to work."

"I make outlines, but I never write them down. I have subconscious outlines that I tap into for direction."

Joyce tends to hear her characters' voices rather than actually visualizing the characters. "I have to work a little harder to see the pictures, how they would say things, how they set their mouths." She says some of her characters are feisty. "I can see them speaking with flashing eyes. I can hear sadness in their voices." Joyce can't always see what her characters are wearing. But that's probably because "I can never figure out what *I'm* wearing! That's just not important to me. How people feel seems to be what I pay most attention to."

Though some authors say they experience writer's block, Joyce doesn't have that problem. "What I have is really more of a 'time block,'" she says. "I'm always trying to find the time to write down all my ideas." Sometimes she gets ideas but doesn't have time to work on them. "That's very frustrating," says Joyce. "I say to myself, 'I wish I could be in my workroom, writing.'"

Joyce grew up in a family of nine children in the small town of Ponca City, Oklahoma, where several of her books are set. She was always reading and writing as a child. "I cannot remember never dreaming or thinking of poems. Writing for me is just like breathing."

The "porch-sitters" she has written about, townspeople who sit on their porches and tell fantastic stories, were very much a part of her childhood. "I grew up hearing those stories," she says. "That's the way people entertained themselves. In certain parts of the country, there are still storytellers."

"I bloom where I am," says Joyce, who has lived in many parts of the United States. "It's what's inside of you that you take with you when you move, not your furniture." Joyce relishes the unexpected in her life. "We will meet different people along this path that we take. We never know what will happen. I walk through life as though there's nothing to fear. If you live your life that way, you're open to good things, even though bad things happen sometimes, too."

JOYCE CAROL THOMAS

When the Nightingale Sings

By the author of National Book Award-winning *Marked by Fire*

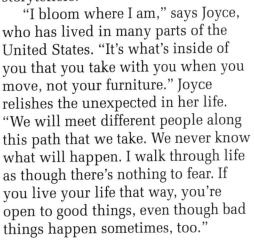

DO IT YOURSELF!

Here is a writing activity from Joyce Carol Thomas: "I always try to teach my students not to take the accepted way of looking at something, but to look deeper. Do not accept what your eyes see or what tradition has told you to believe. If you look deeper, you might come up with an entirely different conclusion than the one you started out with." For example, think about a rock. A rock has not always been a rock. If it is a sedimentary rock, it once might have been a plant, or an animal. Try to look at a familiar object in an unfamiliar way. Write about the object from this different point of view.

Cynthia Voigt

BORN: February 25, 1942, in Boston, Massachusetts
HOME: Penobscot Bay, Maine

SELECTED TITLES

Homecoming
1981

Dicey's Song
(Newbery Medal)
1982

The Callender Papers
1983

Building Blocks
1984

Jackaroo
1985

The Runner
1985

Come a Stranger
1986

Izzy, Willy-Nilly
1986

Stories about Rosie
1987

Sons From Afar
1988

Seventeen Against the Dealer
1989

David and Jonathan
1992

Orfe
1992

The Wings of a Falcon
1993

When Cynthia Voigt gets an idea for a book, she writes it down and walks away. "I see how loudly it calls after me," she says. "Then I leave it alone to grow all by itself. If I can't forget it, I'm probably going to write about it." Not all of Cynthia's ideas pan out. "Some really stink. They just don't come up alive." Letting the ideas develop by themselves in her subconscious, without forcing them or rushing them, lets them "grow their own shape," Cynthia says.

By the time she's ready to write a new book, Cynthia usually has an outline for the whole story in her head. "It's like seeing an architectural design," she says. When she studies the story's structure, "I can see its shape, and I can see where it's weak or where it's out of balance." She remembers reading that the poet Emily Dickinson once wrote, "When ideas are naked, you can tell the good ones from the bad ones. When the clothes are on, they're lost." So Cynthia studies an outline for a good, long time to make sure it's going to hold up under the weight of her story.

WRITING TO DISCOVER

Cynthia is convinced that an important part of writing is discovery. "I write a paragraph and then I say to myself, 'I didn't know I had that idea,'" she says. She believes writing should be "an egotistically delightful task."

A former teacher, Cynthia compares starting a new book with the first few weeks of a new school year.

"The first six weeks of every class, I was always hesitant. I couldn't trust my instincts. I hadn't been there long enough. After that time, I relaxed. If I made a mistake by then, I knew it was just a mistake. The same is true with a story. You have to spend time making false starts, errors in judgment, hating it, not liking it." Cynthia thinks that writing and teaching are very similar occupations. "In both cases, you're doing the same thing over and over again, and the experience is different every time."

Cynthia writes "in a wonderful room," a study on the second floor of an old house. "The ceiling starts high and the walls start low. The room looks out over a garden, and woods beyond that. The windows that look out the other way face a cemetery—the best kind of neighbors to have."

She keeps around her little "totemic objects relevant to the project I'm working on." The totemic object that kept her company while she wrote her newest book, *Wings of a Falcon*, is an ancient model of a falcon that she bought several years ago. "It's black and obsidian and mute and birdlike and tiny," says Cynthia, who says she likes having objects around her "that resonate."

Cynthia likes to write each morning, sometimes breaking up her sessions with exercise or household tasks. Revision is a part of her process. "I assume that the way it looks the day I finish it is not the same way it will look four months down the road." Years ago, her editor at Atheneum told her, "The great thing is not so much to love to write as to learn to love revision." When she first started writing, Cynthia used to think that "smart people didn't make rough drafts or revise, the same way smart people knew the biggest words." Now, she says, she knows both those assumptions were foolhardy.

"I have the most willing suspension of disbelief east of the Alleghenies."

Once she accepts the need for revision of a manuscript, Cynthia enjoys the process. "It's hard and satisfying in a different way than writing." When she's writing something, Cynthia says she's always anxious that the story might not be working. But when she's revising it, she knows she's polishing a story that has already succeeded to a certain degree. "I look it over and try to figure out how to make it clearer." She enjoys tinkering with favorite sentences and scenes. "It's very sensual," says Cynthia. "I just took my latest work down about 40 pages by squeezing out a word here and a word there."

Sometimes there are pictures in Cynthia's mind when she writes, but more often, she hears voices. Sometimes she just tunes out her conscious mind altogether, and lets her fingers type words that come from deep within her. "My fingers know what they're doing," she says. "I leave them alone."

Cynthia says she doesn't "do" writer's block. "When I feel like I'm in trouble I tend to write fast." As she writes fast, she tells herself, "This is all I'm asking you to do today. If you write one paragraph, we'll go out and buy you a present." Usually, that's all the motivation it takes to get past a stuck point.

Cynthia thinks that kids who like to write should make friends with good readers, because it's important to have good advisors. "Some people have a hard time being direct," she says. "You want someone who will be direct and concrete."

She advises teachers who want their students to become good writers "to read their students' writing with full respect." That is because "students write when they see they can get something out of it. If they're not getting interesting feedback, they won't—and maybe even shouldn't— write."

Cynthia believes writers write to discover what they think. "You discover things about yourself," she says. "If you write only to be yourself, that will be your best writing."

DO IT YOURSELF!

Here is a writing activity from Cynthia Voigt: "Take the first sentence of the next book you were going to read. Write your own story based on that sentence. Then read the book."

Laurence Yep

BORN: June 14, 1948, in San Francisco, California
HOME: San Francisco, California

SELECTED TITLES

Dragonwings
(Newbery Honor Book)
1975

Child of the Owl
1977

Dragon of the Lost Sea
1982

Dragon Steel
1985

Shadow Lord
1985

Rainbow People
(reteller)
1989

Dragon Cauldron
1991

Lost Garden
1991

The Star Fisher
1991

Tongues of Jade
1991

American Dragons
1993

Dragon's Gate
1993

The Man Who Tricked a Ghost
1993

Laurence Yep says he's a pretty tough critic of his own work. "I've written 12 drafts of some stories, and six drafts of most novels. With *Dragonwings* [Laurence's award-winning book, written between 1970 and 1974, about a Chinese boy whose father invents an airplane], the number of drafts was a yard high." Laurence has just finished a book about the 19th-century Chinese experience of building the transcontinental railroad. He started working on the book, which is called *Dragon's Gate*, at the same time as *Dragonwings*. Why did it take him so long to finish it? It took a very long time to track down the necessary historical information. Also, he wanted to be sure it would be a very different book from *Dragonwings*. "I didn't want to write 'Dragonwings Builds the Railroad.'"

When Laurence writes, he sometimes feels as if he is looking through a window and telling what he's seeing outside. Images often shoot into his mind. "I just finished writing a book called *Fairybones*," he says. "It's an offshoot of a play I wrote about a healer who goes into the dream world to rescue people who are sick or in a coma. The story began with a scene I imagined of an old lady with her little wagon of cures, walking down a country lane." When he wrote *Dragonwings*, says Laurence, "I could really see that airplane flying." When writing *Dragon's Gate*, Laurence vividly imagined the Chinese railroad workers who were caught in the worst

blizzard of the century while working in the Sierra Nevada mountains. "There was snow 20 feet high," says Laurence. "They lived underneath the snow and walked through tunnels. These Chinese were recruited from Southern China, which is like tropical Mexico. It was like taking a Mexican peasant and sticking him in the middle of a blizzard, without proper clothes."

SWITCHING LENSES

With each book he writes, Laurence imagines himself looking through a different lens. "I got that idea from an actor," he says. "He talks about every role he plays as a kind of lens, so that when he's Willy Loman in *Death of a Salesman*, he can only see people's pain. When he's Iago in *Othello*, he's always looking at everybody else's angles, trying to see what's in it for them. Most of my narratives are first person. Whatever character I am, I look through the lens of the self."

Sometimes Laurence's identification with his characters

actually changes his personality for the period of time he's writing about them. "When I was writing my *Dragon* books, my wife said I was very dragonish," he says. "When I was writing Mark Twain books, I was always very cynical, always going for the punch line."

> ## "I think of my outlines as the scaffolding around a ship. I build the ship from the ground up."

Laurence read a lot as a child—a lot of comic books. "That was how I learned to read," he says. "My parents read me comic books. I would read the comic book story back to them. When I actually found the library, all my skills were in place." At the library he discovered the L. Frank Baum series of *Oz* books. "In the *Oz* books, kids are carried away to a faraway place with strange new customs. They have to adjust to survive." That reminded Laurence of his own life: "I lived in a black neighborhood and went to school in Chinatown. Every time I got on and off the bus, I had to adjust my reality. As a result, I feel like I could be dropped any place on earth."

Laurence once thought he would be a chemist when he grew up. "My father wanted to be a chemist, but the Depression came along, and he had to quit school. He picked fruit and held odd jobs. My ambition was to carry on his ambition." This plan held until Laurence had an English teacher in high school who encouraged students to write for publication. "The teacher said if we got a story accepted by a national publication, we'd get an A in the class. I got bitten by the bug. I kept sending stories out." He sold his first story when he was a freshman in college, to a science-fiction magazine.

He hopes that all those who want to learn to write set aside a definite time and place to do the writing. "You should learn to use all your senses when you write," says Laurence. "Don't just use visual information. Use smells and sounds, because that helps make the writing more vivid. I think of writing as a way of seeing. It's a way of bringing out the specialness of ordinary things. All you really need to do is take a step to the side. Look at the world from a different angle. This gives freshness to your writing and will make it vivid." To Laurence, to be a writer is to "restore your sense of wonder."

DRAGONWINGS
by Laurence Yep

DO IT YOURSELF!

Here is a writing activity from Laurence Yep: "For several minutes, close your eyes and just breathe. Listen to the world around you. Try to map it by sounds. It's a totally different world when you do that. After several minutes, open your eyes and look at something right in front of you. It's a simple little trick. If your eyes are deprived of visual data for a few minutes, they will be almost starved. They will focus on anything and look at it hungrily. You'll notice the light shimmering across your desk, or the steam rising from a cup of coffee. Write down what you see."

Celebrating Authors and Illustrators

SETTING UP AN AUTHOR/ILLUSTRATOR CENTER

Imagine you are visiting from a foreign land. In a matter of minutes, simply by glancing around, you can easily identify the kinds of things that are valued in the culture you are visiting.

For example: an outdoor sculpture suggests an appreciation of art; playing fields indicate a love for sports and fitness; statues of statespeople show a respect for leadership. The same can be said for our classrooms. Take a look around. What do we, as teachers, value? What messages, however subtle, are we sending to our "foreign visitors"— the students for whom these very rooms exist?

If we hang student writing or art on the walls, we are saying to children that we value their creativity. If shelves of children's books line our walls, we show our love for reading and literature. The classroom environment we create does much more than facilitate learning—it expresses our values, ideals, and ambitions for our students.

With this in mind, here are a few tips to help you set up author/illustrator centers:

- The most important thing is space. Allocate plenty of space for books, complete with cozy reading areas. This shows that reading is a valued activity.

- Set up a table upon which, each week or every couple of weeks, you highlight a particular author or illustrator. This table might include work by the author or illustrator, a photo, and letters to that person from students or the class.

- Encourage the class to write to publishers requesting information about favorite authors or illustrators. You may receive informational brochures, photos, bibliographies, or even newspaper clippings.

- Display student projects that tie into the creators' books. They can be drawings, related science projects, research papers, poems, stories, or whatever.

CELEBRATING BIRTHDAYS

As a nation, we celebrate the birthdays of Abraham Lincoln, George Washington, and Martin Luther King, Jr. Why not, as a classroom, celebrate Mem Fox's or Jerry Spinelli's? By celebrating a creator's birthday, we reflect on and commemorate his or her contribution to literature.

Here are a few tips for celebrating authors' and illustrators' birthdays in your classroom:

- For the week prior to the celebration, set up a table that displays the author's or illustrator's work and any biographical information you may have.

- On the big day, be sure to share plenty of the author's or illustrator's work with the class.

- Send the author or illustrator a birthday card. You might want to brainstorm together to think of an appropriate class gift for the author. Jan Brett, the author and illustrator of *The Mitten*, might appreciate some mittens, for example.

- Ask students to bring in items related to the events, characters, or settings of the books. If your celebrated author/illustrator is Lois Ehlert, students might bring in some of the foods mentioned in *Eating the Alphabet* for everyone to share; if your celebrated author is Sid Fleischman, who is a magician, students might bring in magic tricks to perform for their classmates.

- You or your students may want to dress up as characters from some of the books. If the book is set in the past, dressing up can really be fun—and very educational.

- The important thing is to let your imagination run wild. Let the students actively contribute ideas. You might even want to serve birthday cake!

ADVENTURING WITH BOOKS

Books are wonderful springboards for all sorts of enjoyable learning activities—from putting on plays to serious class discussions, from creative writing to cooperative art projects. The important thing is to recognize the tremendous possibilities in good books. You've already captured student interest. Now you can build on that motivation by exploring further.

EXTENSION ACTIVITIES

Here are some book-related activities you might want to try with the class:

Character Biographies

Invite students to write brief biographies of storybook characters. Encourage your students to make up details that weren't in the story but seem to fit the character. Illustrations are welcome too.

Story Patterns

A great way to help students appreciate the structure of stories is to recognize and imitate the patterns of their favorite books. With a little guidance, kids can do this with almost every book—from alphabet and counting books to more sophisticated folktales.

A Familiar Character in a New Situation

By reading, kids can "get to know" a character. You can put this knowledge to the test by asking students to put a familiar character in a totally new situation. Authors tell us that many stories are created by using this simple technique.

Writing Nonfiction

It's helpful for kids to realize that different types of books "do" different things. Nonfiction books, such as Gail Gibbons's *How a House Is Built*, give factual information. Ask students to write a nonfiction book, such as *How to Care for Tropical Fish* if they have a household or class pet, or *How to Use the Library* or *A Day in the Life of Our Town*.

Interviews

The information about authors in this book is largely based on interviews. Students can interview each other, relatives, and community members. They first need to decide what they want to learn and make a list of questions. They may wish to capture the interview on an audio- or videotape recorder.

Joke and Riddle Books

Here's another form of writing kids can pursue. It may take some research, such as asking classmates and friends if they've heard any good jokes. They may want to team up with an artist who can illustrate the jokes. When creating this type of book, students become editors: they decide which jokes to include and where, and they help the illustrator come up with funny ideas.

Plays

When books feature lots of action and dialogue, they can easily be adapted to play form. Get students to write their own adaptations and then perform them. For the most fun, designate class members to be responsible for costumes, playbills, tickets—the works!

Illustrations

Some stories, such as classic folktales, lend themselves to many interpretations. Encourage students who exhibit an interest in art to respond to folktales by illustrating one. They should begin by writing out the text, without any pictures at all. Then they'll need to decide how many words go on each page. They may begin, like professional illustrators, by making rough sketches before the final versions. Other students can help out as editors.

For Homework . . . Forget Your Homework!

As you know, kids are often most creative when trying to explain why they didn't do their homework. You can turn this talent to advantage by giving the following assignment: "Today's homework is to make up a really good excuse for not doing your homework—the wilder the excuse, the better." You may want to gather and illustrate these stories in one collection: "Room 213's Book of Outrageous Excuses!"

What Happens Next?

Have students write sequels to beloved books. Kids understand this concept from movie sequels, so the assignment is the same: give us another story or adventure featuring the same character. They'll need to go back and look closely at the key elements of the first story, trying to incorporate similar elements into their new book.

> **NOTE:** Remember, the primary purpose of literature is to give pleasure to the reader. Not every book or story necessarily has to be followed by a series of activities. Sometimes it's best to read a story aloud, close the cover, smile, and simply say, "Wasn't that wonderful!"

AUTHORS' AND ILLUSTRATORS' BIRTHDAYS

Month/Day		Month/Day	
1/4	Phyllis Reynolds Naylor	7/28	Natalie Babbitt
1/29	Rosemary Wells	8/1	Gail Gibbons
1/30	Tony Johnston	8/6	Barbara Cooney
2/1	Jerry Spinelli	8/9	Patricia McKissack
2/3	Joan Lowery Nixon	8/12	Ann M. Martin
2/7	Shonto Begay	8/25	Lane Smith
2/25	Cynthia Voigt	8/28	J. Brian Pinkney
3/5	Mem Fox	8/28	Allen Say
3/16	Sid Fleischman	9/8	Jack Prelutsky
3/20	Bill Martin, Jr.	9/21	Hans Wilhelm
4/2	Ruth Heller	9/12	Kevin Major
4/6	Graeme Base	9/16	Joanne Ryder
4/26	Patricia Reilly Giff	9/27	Paul Goble
5/3	Mavis Jukes	10/8	Faith Ringgold
5/11	Peter Sis	10/9	Johanna Hurwitz
5/15	Norma Fox Mazer	10/11	Russell Freedman
5/16	Bruce Coville	11/3	Bette Bao Lord
5/17	Eloise Greenfield	11/9	Lois Ehlert
5/25	Ann McGovern	11/12	Marjorie Weinman Sharmat
5/25	Joyce Carol Thomas	11/15	Daniel Pinkwater
6/1	Doris Buchanan Smith	11/16	Robin McKinley
6/6	Peter Spier	11/24	Gloria Houston
6/14	Laurence Yep	11/25	Marc Brown
6/24	Kathryn Lasky	12/1	Jan Brett
6/24	Jean Marzollo	12/9	Joan Blos
6/26	Charlotte Zolotow	12/19	Eve Bunting
6/28	Bette Greene	12/20	Lulu Delacre
7/2	Jean Craighead George	12/28	Cynthia DeFelice
7/11	Patricia Polacco	12/28	Janet Lunn
7/17	Karla Kuskin	12/30	Jane Langton

ACKNOWLEDGMENTS

Thanks to the authors who opened their doors and let us in. Thanks to publishing people who went out of their way, especially William Morris at HarperCollins and Maria Sinopoli at Scholastic. Thanks to great librarians, especially Lucy Evankow of Scholastic and the staff at the Southworth Library in South Dartmouth, Massachusetts. Thanks to dedicated booksellers, in particular Frank Hodge of Hodge-Podge in Albany, New York, and Carol Chittenden and Betty Borg at Eight Cousins in Falmouth, Massachusetts. Thanks to book-loving teachers like Virginia Kuhn and great readers like Rachel and Eliza Burnes. Thanks to James Preller for his sympathetic ear and many helpful suggestions and to insightful editors Terry Cooper and Liza Schafer. Special thanks to Claudia Cohl, for her lasting support. Thanks most of all to Niko, who has always been there.

–D.K.

Thanks to Terry Cooper, Frank Hodge, William Morris, Deborah Kovacs, and Liza Schafer. And special thanks to Maria, through thick and thin.

–J.P.

BIBLIOGRAPHY

Almost all of the material in this book was obtained through direct interviews with the authors and illustrators. In many cases, however, additional biographical material was supplied by their publishers or found in relevant books and articles. The Something About the Author *series (Gale Research) was an especially helpful resource.*

RESOURCE MATERIALS ON SPECIFIC AUTHORS

Natalie Babbitt
Babbitt, Natalie. "About Patricia MacLachlan." *Horn Book*, July/August 1986.
————. "Metamorphosis." *Horn Book*, September/October 1988.
————. "The Rhinocerous and the Pony." *Horn Book*, November/December 1989.
————. "Who Is the Child?" *Horn Book*, March/April 1986.

Shonto Begay
Elleman, Barbara. "Shonto Begay's *The Mud Pony*." *Book Links*, July 1992.
Villiani, John. "Navajo Painter Shonto Begay Talks About Two Diverse Worlds." *The New Mexican*, September 13, 1991.

Joan Blos
Kingman, Lee, ed. *Newbery and Caldecott Medal Books: 1976–1985*. Horn Book, 1986.

Jan Brett
"Jan Brett." A Scholastic Author Tape, Scholastic, 1991.

Barbara Cooney
"Barbara Cooney." The Trumpet Club Authors on Tape, Bantam, 1989.

Lois Ehlert
"Lois Ehlert." A Scholastic Author Tape, Scholastic, 1992.

Mem Fox
Fox, Mem. *Dear Mem Fox, I Have Read All Your Books Even the Pathetic Ones*. Harcourt Brace Jovanovich, 1992.

Sid Fleischman
Kingman, Lee, ed. *Newbery and Caldecott Medal Books: 1976–1985*. Horn Book, 1986.

Russell Freedman
Freedman, Russell. "Newbery Medal Acceptance Speech." *Horn Book*, August/September 1987.
————. "Pursuing the Pleasure Principle." *Horn Book*, January/February 1986.

Jean Craighead George
Kingman, Lee, ed. *Newbery and Caldecott Medal Books: 1976–1985*. Horn Book, 1986.

Patricia Reilly Giff
"Patricia Reilly Giff." The Trumpet Club Authors on Tape, Bantam, 1992.

Paul Goble
Goble, Paul. "On Beaded Dresses and the Blazing Sun," *The Native American Folktale*, 1991.

Eloise Greenfield
Prelutsky, Jack. "Jack Prelutsky's Poetry Pages: Eloise Greenfield." *Instructor*, February 1993.

Ruth Heller
"Ruth Heller." A Scholastic Author Tape, Scholastic, 1992.

Kathryn Lasky
Lasky, Kathryn. "Creating in a Boom Industry." *Horn Book*, November/December 1991.
————. "Reflections on Nonfiction." *Horn Book*, September/October 1985.

Bill Martin, Jr.
"Bill Martin, Jr. and John Archambault," The Trumpet Club Authors on Tape, Bantam, 1990.

J. Brian Pinkney
Evans, Dilys. "Four African American Illustrators," *Book Links*, January 1993.

Patricia Polacco
Maughan, Shannon. "Patricia Polacco." *Publishers Weekly*, February 15, 1993.
Lewis, Valerie. "Patricia Polacco." *Instructor*, April, 1993.

Naylor, Phyllis Reynolds
Naylor, Phyllis Reynolds. "Newbery Medal Acceptance Speech." *Horn Book*, September/November 1992.

Faith Ringgold
"Faith Ringgold." A Scholastic Author Tape, Scholastic, 1993.
Raymond, Allen. "Faith Ringgold: 'It's Like Being a Kid All Over Again!'" *Teaching K–8*, March 1993.
Fenly, Leigh. "Artist Lets Dreams of Freedom Take Wing." *The San Diego Union*, February 16, 1991.

Slesin, Suzanne. "Quilts That Warm in New Ways." *The New York Times*, December 6, 1990.

Fox, Catherine. "Ringgold's Art Tells Stories, Topples Barriers." *The Atlanta Constitution*, July 30, 1990.

Flomenhaft, Eleanor. "Faith Ringgold: A 25 Year Survey." Fine Arts Museums of Long Island, n.d.

Allen Say

"Allen Say." A Scholastic Author Tape, Scholastic, 1992.

Peter Sis

Sis, Peter. "The Artist at Work." *Horn Book*, November/December 1992.

Lane Smith

Zvirin, Stephanie. "The Booklist Interview: Jon Scieszka and Lane Smith." *Booklist*, September 1, 1992.

Smith, Amanda. "Jon Scieszka and Lane Smith." *Publishers Weekly*, July 26, 1991.

Smith, Lane. "The Artist at Work." *Horn Book*, January/February 1993.

Peter Spier

"Peter Spier." The Trumpet Club Authors on Tape, Bantam, 1989.

Jerry Spinelli

Spinelli, Jerry. "Newbery Medal Acceptance Speech." *Horn Book*, August/September 1991.

Cynthia Voigt

Kingman, Lee, ed. *Newbery and Caldecott Medal Books: 1976–1985*. Horn Book, 1986.

Rosemary Wells

Wells, Rosemary. "Words & Pictures: The Right Order." *Publishers Weekly*, February 27, 1987.

——. "Shy Charles." *Horn Book*, January/February 1990.

——. "The Artist at Work: The Writer at Work." *Horn Book*, March/ April 1987.

Laurence Yep

"Thoughts on the Importance of Children's Versions of History." *Horn Book*, May/June 1989.

PHOTO CREDITS

DEBORAH KOVACS is the author of many books for children, including *A Day Underwater* (Scholastic), *Brewster's Courage* (Simon & Schuster), and *Moonlight on the River* (Viking). She lives in Massachusetts with her husband and two children.

JAMES PRELLER is the author of several books for children, including *How to Play Little League Baseball* (Kidsbooks, 1991) and *Wake Me in Spring* (Scholastic, 1994). He lives in Albany, New York, with his wife, Maria, son, Nicholas, and dog, Doolin.

Be sure to look for volume one of *Meet the Authors and Illustrators*. This companion collection is also by Deborah Kovacs and James Preller. It includes profiles of Eric Carle, Tomie dePaola, Jane Yolen, Beverly Cleary, Walter Dean Meyers, and 55 other very special creators of children's books.

ISBN 49097 $19.95   144 pages